Beauty & Convenience

Beauty & Convenience

ARCHITECTURE AND
ORDER IN THE NEW REPUBLIC

Nora Pat Small

THE UNIVERSITY OF TENNESSEE PRESS / Knoxville

Copyright © 2003 by The University of Tennessee Press / Knoxville.
All Rights Reserved. Manufactured in the United States of America.
First Edition.

This book is printed on acid-free paper.

Library of Congress Cataloging-in-Publication Data

Small, Nora Pat.
Beauty and convenience: architecture and order in the
new republic / Nora Pat Small.— 1st ed.
    p. cm.
Includes bibliographical references and index.

ISBN 1-57233-236-0 (cl. alk. paper)

  1. Farmhouses—New England.
  2. Farm buildings—New England.
  3. Architecture, Domestic—New England.
  4. Architecture—New England—19th century.
  5. Neoclassicism (Architecture)—New England.
  6. Architecture and society—New England.
  I. Title: Architecture and order in the new republic.
  II. Title.

NA8208.52.N48 S63 2003
728'.37'097409034—dc21   2003005697

To Nora-ma and Kerm

Contents

Figures

Maps

Acknowledgments

I have Tom Hubka to thank for starting all this. He organized a fascinating little conference in conjunction with the publication of his book *Big House, Little House, Back House, Barn* that introduced me to a rural New England that I had never really seen, although I had certainly looked at it frequently enough. At that conference I met Sally McMurry, whose probing questions then, and insightful comments later on my dissertation, spurred me on to look ever more closely at the material and archival evidence before me. Without that conference I doubt I would have seen Sutton, Massachusetts—to which my husband, daughter, and I moved in 1988—in the same way.

The quintessential New England picturesqueness of the place was irresistible, but thanks to several local historians it soon became much more than pretty scenery. Bud Gurney seemed to know everyone who had ever lived in Sutton, could explain who was related to whom, and could show me where their houses, mills, and schools had been or still were. Without Bud, Malcolm Pearson, Ruth Putnam, Ben MacLaren, and Donna MacLaren Rossio, much of the local archival and material evidence would have remained mute. Among them they could identify every mystery photograph and cellar hole, and bring them to life with their stories. They know far more about this place than I could ever encompass in a single book.

Early in my fieldwork, it was my great good fortune to stop at the house owned by Elizabeth and Ned Bacon. Their enthusiastic reception of my request to look into every nook and cranny of their house and to spend at least one day dragging a tape measure around it, gave me courage to knock on more doors. I owe a debt of gratitude to all of those who allowed me to intrude on them and their houses. They are too numerous to name here. I was privileged in the course of my fieldwork to spend time with Mary King, Leona Dona, and the Stevensons, whose hospitality and knowledge of Sutton they shared freely. Measuring, drawing, and just looking at old buildings is much easier with an extra pair of hands and eyes. Susan Ceccacci, Martha McNamara, and Jeanne Whitney all provided that extra help. Working with Myron Stachiw and Tom Paske on a couple of other projects for Old Sturbridge Village provided me an invaluable opportunity to sharpen my fieldwork and observation skills, and to make sense of what I saw in Sutton.

Some people helped this project along unwittingly, by just being there. Jane Donovan and Elizabeth Bacon provided invaluable assistance in that manner. My family has been a source of much needed support and distraction. Rick has gone above and beyond by assisting with graphics and computer problems.

This book began as a dissertation under the direction of Robert St. George, who suggested I apply for admission to the American and New England Studies Program at Boston University. I remain in his debt for that push back into the academy. As a Midwesterner, I thought everything already had been written about New England. Bob, Richard Candee, and Alan Taylor all tried their best to get me to think critically and analytically about the buildings, their historical context and the relevant historiography. Any shortcomings in this work are my own doing. In the course of conducting research it was my privilege to spend many hours at the American Antiquarian Society in Worcester, Massachusetts. I thank the fine staff there, especially Joanne Chaison, for all they do to make obscure archives accessible.

Finally, I thank all the Donna Rossios of the world, who fight to preserve the special character and history of places like Sutton.

Introduction

In the half-century following the American Revolution rural New Englanders transformed their built environment. They reordered houses, barns, and fields in accordance with newly popular and widespread notions of beauty and convenience; they created commercial and social town centers where none had existed before; they dammed their rivers and streams and built textile mills and machine shops containing water-powered machinery. In doing so they adapted old building forms to new uses, and even created new forms. They clung to tradition and embraced innovation as they rebuilt or broke ground for new homesteads, barnyards, villages, and mill sites. Evident yet in the miles of stone walls, in the farmhouses, barns, mills, and churches that lie thick on the landscape, this rebuilding serves as the basis for most Americans' visual or mental image of rural New England. Seemingly colonial and classical at the same time, the landscape appears time-less, natural, unspoiled (fig. 1). Architectural historians have long recognized this flurry of building activity as a significant period in American architectural history, but few scholars have examined the phenomenon closely. Some have even dismissed the significance of this era of rebuilding entirely. Although he did not comment on the intensity of building activity, Fiske Kimball observed that the Revolution "brought a fundamental change in American domestic architecture," an assessment that other scholars might agree with if modified with "for the middle and upper class." The rebuilding is undeniable, but its overall effect on housing in the new republic can be overstated if we forget how much poor and substandard housing remained that has left no trace on the landscape today.[1] This work will focus on what *was* rebuilt, by whom and in what manner. Although rooted in colonial practice and classical precedent, the landscape that resulted from this rebuilding was also something brand new, far from timeless, natural or unspoiled. The result of specific cultural, economic, social, and industrial conditions, picture-post-card New England blossomed amidst controversy, noise, and tumult.

This study of the reordering of the central Massachusetts countryside in the first generation of the new republic is predicated on three beliefs. First, buildings, and objects in general, can be read as texts and should be considered as primary documents. Field work reveals patterns, continuities, and discontinuities in past building practice. Second, texts are slippery things that change meaning as physical and historical contexts change, as we become removed, that is, from their origins in space and time. We need look no further than the building forms that embodied beauty and convenience in the early nineteenth century, which came to be seen as unaesthetic boxes by the middle of that century, to see the truth in that. Third, objects or landscapes and written documents need to be studied in conjunction with one another to be fully understood. Rural reformers aimed to impose certain standards on a real landscape. Their admonitions against overbuilding and acquiring the "false taste" of the city, and their promotions of economy and natural ornaments can be interpreted as mere rhetoric, as an abstract and timeless call to

Fig. 1 View of West Sutton, the quintessential New England landscape. Stone walls border farm fields and roads. Houses and fields seemingly cluster about the church in the middle landscape. From Benedict and Tracy, *History of the Town of Sutton.*

republican virtue, until we observe the rural built landscape. Then it is apparent that their distress arose from actual conditions, and equally apparent that they viewed developments in the countryside from quite a different perspective than did the inhabitants of that countryside.

Understanding the reasons for innovative or customary construction and design requires placing those buildings within the social and cultural context in which they were created. In so doing we discover how unperceptive our modern-day reading of artifacts can be, and how much of an object's meaning can be lost or distorted as the specific forces that coalesced around its creation dissipate. We also discover that using objects and written documents together as primary sources reveals meanings in a landscape or an era that are irretrievable otherwise.

The predominance of old two-story houses in rural New England at the end of the nineteenth century has resulted in a skewed perception of typical New England building practices. The misconception of New England's ancient farmhouses beginning as two-story, five-bay, rambling structures has begun to be redressed in the last twenty years in works by Abbott Lowell Cummings, Michael Steinitz, and Thomas Hubka.[2] Cummings demonstrated that over half of the first period (pre-1725) houses he studied grew to their center-chimney, two-story form over time.[3] Hubka found that the big house, little house, back house, barn form associated with traditional practice in New England was largely a nineteenth-century phenomenon. He concluded that New England's fully connected farm buildings reached the height of their popularity and attained acceptance by reformers around 1850. Acknowledging the connected house and barn as the "symbol of progressive agricultural improvement in New England,"[4] he mistakenly interprets the ells that connected dwelling and barn as elements of folk building, a longstanding practice among rural New Englanders. But research in Sutton suggests a more recent origin for the widespread use of ells among non-gentry. Joseph Wood has argued that the New England central village developed between 1790 and 1820 due to improvements in agricultural production, transportation networks, communication, and manufacturing, rather than during the colonial era with which it was associated early in the twentieth century.[5] To this interpretation we can add that the two-story, bilaterally symmetrical dwelling with ell that has come to epitomize New England building took hold in the post-Revolution era of village building, a product of that self-proclaimed age of improvement's zeal for beauty and convenience. Although some gentry built rural seats with ells or wings just prior to the Revolution, the practice remained uncommon in rural communities until around the turn of the eighteenth century. For the rural rebuilders, ells embodied not just economic aspirations and achievements, but participation in a broader culture that demanded efficiency and convenience in all facets of life.

As rural New Englanders rebuilt their landscape, they provoked the ire of a group of predominantly urban, self-proclaimed rural reformers. The classically detailed, two-story-with-ell houses that to present-day viewers look traditional or commonplace, engendered moral outrage among the reformers at the time of their construction. The disjunction between our perception of these buildings and contemporary commentators' assessments indicates that a significant level of meaning, the original intention of the builders, has been lost. Just as buildings acquire layers of paint and wallpaper and are added to and reduced, so too do they acquire new layers of meaning through time, or lose their meaning altogether in societies that can no longer fathom their original purposes or create a new one. A seventeenth-century farmhouse converted to a hay barn in the nineteenth century and demolished in the twentieth obviously underwent a series of changes in the way it was perceived, in its meaning to its users. Because of accretion or loss of material and meaning, it is often difficult to recognize the original intentions of a structure's builder and user. When we can no longer fathom the cause of reformers' animosity toward seemingly innocuous farmhouses, then we have lost track of cultural forces that can help us define and comprehend the early republic. The breach between what the arbiters of taste declared was appropriate or inappropriate for rural habitations and what was actually built is the beginning point for unearthing layers of meaning.

Whether one perceived architectural developments in the countryside with alarm or satisfaction all depended on viewpoint. This work will examine the points of view from which contemporaries viewed the transformation of the New England countryside. It will begin with the view from the outside, nearly a bird's-eye view, that of the primarily urban-based rural reformers and scientific farmers. Eighteenth- and nineteenth-century historians, philosophers, and scientists viewed the history of the world as the history of the progress of civilization from east to west. The new United States stood in line to be the next home of the muses of art and science, to assume a position of world leadership in all matters, be they political, economic, or cultural. The evidence of this preeminent place of the new republic would lie in its cultural attainments, in particular in its architectural accomplishments. Careful reading of the texts condemning rural building practice reveals that the source of the animosity toward these dwellings lay not in the form of the buildings, a form used widely by the gentry, but in who was constructing them and where they were being constructed. Reformers based their condemnations on two compatible philosophies—one political and the other aesthetic. The first, primarily a metaphorical device derived from classical traditions, held that a nation's virtue resided in its farmers. The second was of more recent origin and was based on aesthetic theories. Rural beauty, according to the ideas of association and appropriateness of mid-eighteenth-century aesthetic theory, rested on an affinity with nature. The two-story Georgian dwelling was an artful, and artificial, construct inappropriate to a common working farmscape.[6] Such dwellings suited urban situations and the rural homes of the gentry who knew how to set off a mansion in an appropriate landscape. Otherwise they were inappropriate for rural sites, especially for the homes of farmers. The problem lay in the fact that at one level of meaning, houses expressed taste, which in the early nineteenth century was taken as a physical manifestation of moral soundness. From the reforming gentry's point of view, the appearance of inappropriate house forms in rural areas was not a simple matter of aesthetics. They saw a rural hinterland being transformed in ways that did not coincide with their urbane vision of republican rectitude, a vision in which the farmer played no small part. Straying from the image of rural beauty that the reformers held, the builders and occupants of these dwellings strayed from virtue as well.

This censure by a group of critics of another group distinct from themselves and judged incapable of understanding the implications or withstanding the consequences of their actions was also mirrored in the criticism of novels in the early republic.[7] The mass consumption of novels that Cathy Davidson observed for this time period is matched by the mass consumption of refined culture that Richard Bushman explored in *The Refinement of America*.[8] Davidson, however, sees novels as a form of communication outside of the classical rhetorical tradition, not emulative of that elite style in spite of some borrowings from traditional literary forms. Bushman, on the other hand, interprets the spread of genteel culture as emulation, as the desire of non-gentility to share in the same power structures, the same refined society, from which they were, in reality, excluded. As will be seen, the physical evidence from Sutton, in conjunction with the printed sources, suggests that new notions of modernity, not emulation, were behind the adoption of new standards of living.

The next viewpoint belongs to that group of architects and master carpenters who wished to influence the broad course of rural building, and who, to that end, published treatises telling rural folk how they should build their homes, churches and meetinghouses, and courthouses. Rather than addressing clients, the pattern book authors aimed their advice directly at rural builders, the ones responsible for erecting new buildings and remodeling old ones. With a thorough knowledge of building practices and technology, they published a plethora of books intended to aid the rural artisan and client in creating modern structures suited to the new republican era. While presenting their readers with the details, and sometimes the overall views and plans, necessary to create visions of beauty and convenience, they seldom directly addressed the uses of the spaces enclosed in these modern structures. And why should they? Custom and necessity dictated where a farmwife performed the myriad of housekeeping chores, food processing and outwork duties for which she was responsible. Artisans and farmers knew better than book authors how to arrange their work spaces. But the authors knew what kind of face the finished product should present to the world, what an upright republican citizen's home should look like. To the architects of the day, beauty and convenience in American architecture indicated the strength and success of the republican experiment. In their architectural system, beauty consisted of the deployment of classical architectural vocabulary in a conveniently arranged building. Asher Benjamin—master carpenter, architect and pattern book author—played a major role in adapting the latest form of classicism to, and disseminating it throughout, the new republic. Following the lead of Benjamin and other leading practitioners and authors, rural builders and architects created a peculiarly American variation on the then modern international style. In the minds of these designers and builders, the new classicism demonstrated the success of the American political experiment.

All of this was well and good for those who could afford to theorize about the proper shape of the landscape. In the meantime, however, people had to live real lives that did not necessarily mesh precisely with political and architectural theory. They had to find ways to earn a competence in the unfamiliar economic, political, and social terrain of a postwar embryonic nation. They reshaped their built environment to accommodate new farming and manufacturing practices, new family composition, and new social structure, and they did so in ways both familiar and new. Enmeshed already in a world of classical traditions, neither the classically inspired rhetoric of the rural reformers nor the neoclassical architecture of the pattern book authors would have seemed in the least bit strange. Both exemplified modern variations on very old themes. Because they already spoke the language, rural New Englanders could use the vocabulary to create their own syntax, to create a modern vernacular, as it were. Just as they were caught up in a world-wide economy beyond their immediate control, and yet managed to play a significant role in shaping the regional economy and thus influencing global trade, so too were these rural residents both responsible for and responsive to modern building tenets.

The last viewpoint, then, belongs to those who transformed southeastern New England's rural landscape after the Revolution. This is the insider's point of view, not what could be or should be, but what was. Unlike the first two groups whose writings speak for them, buildings and the landscape speak for these people. The old adage of actions speaking louder than words applies here. The words of the rural reformers and the pattern book authors engage only a few scholars with specialized interests these days, but the results of the rebuilding of the early republic still confront and engage thousands of people on a daily basis. The problem is that most of us cannot read the landscape as easily as words on a page, so we decipher it in terms with which we are familiar. It is pretty, or quaint, or old fashioned, it is frozen in time, it is decrepit, but for the casual observer, it is not a political statement or the logical result of work patterns or a response to changing social and economic structures. In asking why this era's rural buildings look the way they do, how they differed from and resembled their predecessors and successors, we confront cultural and social systems and beliefs that undergirded the built environment—the politics, economics, demographics, taste, and customary practices that determined the final choice of form and style.

A reliance on classical tenets, whether literary or architectural, united all of these viewpoints. It ran through all of the discussions, as allegory or as model. Rural reformers assumed that their audiences—farmers and gentlemen alike—would understand not only their references to the classical orders, but also their repeated references to the yeomanry as the seat of virtue. Asher Benjamin did not have to argue for classicism as the best style, it was the only style, the *true* style. The only question was how the orders should be used, not whether they should be used. Builders, architects, and their clients all spoke the language of classical architecture, although they often expressed themselves in a local idiom. The country men and women who surrounded themselves with classical forms lived in a world replete with classical references. Throughout the revolutionary years they read essays or broadsides signed by Cato and others of Roman lineage, and understood the associations between their fight against tyranny and the ancients' similar battles. The ideals of the classical republic informed daily discourse well into the nineteenth century. Newspaper subscribers, whose numbers grew rapidly in post-Revolution New England, regularly encountered essays that in one way or another referred to classical republicanism. The spirit of Cincinnatus lived on, so the rhetoric went, in this new country where farmers had set aside their plows to fight for freedom, and then had returned to those plows. Contrary to Richard Bushman's argument in *The Refinement of America,* these middling sorts did not adopt, or even emulate, an aristocratic culture when they chose to build two-story, classically detailed farmhouses with parlors. It was not the leisured and courtly culture of the elite that these people adopted, which Bushman points out did not set well with people given to "hard work and parsimonious habits," but the vocabulary—a vocabulary that represented republican ideals rather than aristocracy.[9]

The landscape of rural New England remains relatively mute until we consider each of these viewpoints and the classical constructs, along with the physical and social realities, in which they were enmeshed. Our point of departure will be the Massachusetts countryside, specifically the town of Sutton. The extant eighteenth- and early-nineteenth-century landscape there serves as the basis for an exploration of the conflicts inherent among reformers' philosophical classicism, builders' architectural classicism, and rural residents' domestic and economic lives. In the domestic and agricultural landscape we see the compromises and disjunctions between the rhetoric of rural reform and agricultural improvement, and the reality of an industrializing, but still agricultural rural economy. The economic interdependence of agriculture and industry, usually treated as discrete pursuits, here assumes physical form. In this place millwrights were farmers, and farmers were artisans, merchants, and gentlemen. Farmhouses contained workrooms, and homesteads contained workshops in which farm men and women produced goods and equipment for local use and for export. The architectural idiom that architectural historians have since labeled neoclassical or Federal defines post-Revolution building in New England because it grew out of these very specific circumstances.

After eighty years of settlement, a national revolution, a local rebellion sanctioned by town vote (known afterwards as Shays' rebellion) and with an industrial revolution brewing, Sutton, Massachusetts, residents embarked on building campaigns that would result, by 1840, in a landscape markedly different from the one with which they had opened the century, yet tied to the earlier era by customary practices that refused to be dislodged. Watered by several rivers and natural ponds, Sutton provided excellent territory for both agricultural pursuits and manufacturing. As this rebuilding began, Sutton had money and power, meaning that its residents could, and did, participate fully in the wholesale transformation of their landscape.

Sutton lies in the Blackstone River valley in the southeast corner of Worcester County, which itself occupies the middle of Massachusetts from north to south (map 1). The Blackstone River valley was at the center of the industrial revolution that followed on the heels of the war for independence (see inset, map 1). The river and its tributaries, already heavily utilized for milling and small-scale manufacturing when the Revolutionary War commenced, were further developed during the war. Investors established a paper mill, a powder mill, and a water-powered armory in Sutton during the war years. The period under discussion here—1790 through the 1830s—began with the arrival of Samuel Slater in Pawtucket, Rhode Island, at the southern end of the valley, and the opening of his textile mills there. This pivotal event in the history of American industry marked a change in scale and product for the manufacturing interests of the Blackstone River valley and not, it should be noted, the sudden intrusion of industry into a purely agricultural landscape.

To the north, at the headwaters of the Blackstone River, Worcester, Massachusetts, partook in the intensification of industry in the valley that followed swiftly on the opening of Slater's mills. It developed into a transportation hub as well as a manufacturing center. Worcester quickly surpassed in size and prominence other county towns, including Sutton, that throughout the eighteenth century had exceeded it in wealth and population. Industrial villages, such as Sutton's Manchaug and Wilkinsonville, lay scattered throughout the valley by 1828, when the Blackstone Canal linking Worcester to Providence was completed. The Boston and Worcester Railroad, completed in 1835, and the Providence and Worcester Railroad, completed in 1847, superseded the transportation advances provided by the canal. Sutton, with both the Blackstone Canal and the Providence and Worcester Railroad running through its northeast corner, felt the impact of these changes.

Caught up in the industrialization of the Blackstone Valley, Sutton thrived in the decades following the founding of the new republic. Population grew steadily throughout the first half of the nineteenth century. Dwellings, barns, and shops all increased in numbers, the most dramatic gains occurring between 1810 and 1830.[10] The stability of Sutton's population and the steady growth in farm buildings and agricultural products in the early nineteenth century indicate that it retained an agricultural base even while its manufacturing neighborhoods grew.

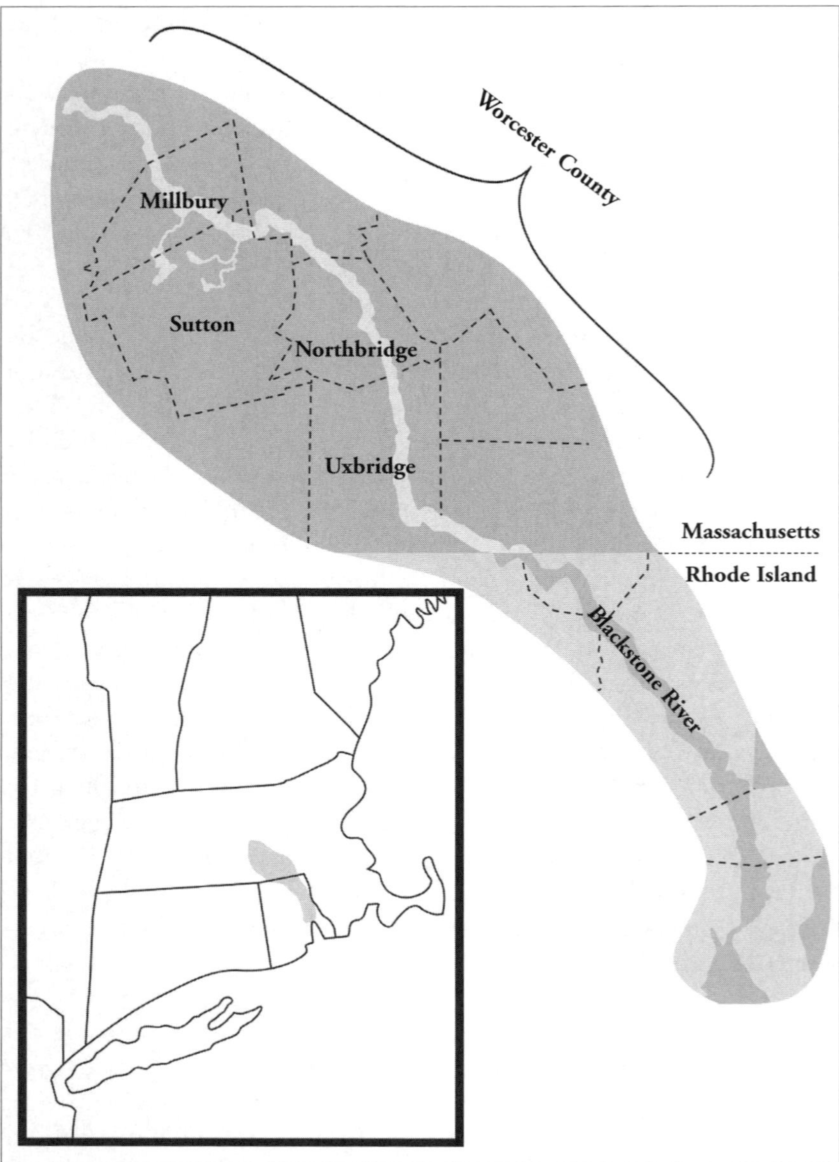

Map 1 | Blackstone River valley with inset showing location in New England. The Blackstone River valley stretches from Providence, Rhode Island, to Worcester, Massachusetts. Prepared by the author and Rick Riccio.

The combination of agricultural and manufacturing pursuits remains evident yet throughout the Blackstone River valley. Physical and archival evidence indicates that the imposition of a new order on fields and yards presaged the reordering of domestic spaces, while a barn form new to the valley emerged more slowly. The timing of the appearance of this New England barn coincides with the industrialization of the valley. Farmers not only produced more agricultural products for the market, they and their families also became enmeshed in outwork systems, all of which demanded that they become attuned to efficiency in production methods.[11] The acceptance of the new barn form is as indicative of farm families' relationships to manufacturing, both in terms of supplying those markets and in terms of work patterns, as it is of the nature of their farm operation.

The continuation of Sutton's agricultural and manufacturing tradition into the 1950s, and even to a lesser extent into the 1990s, ensured the survival of much of the nineteenth-century landscape, as field boundaries, road systems, and manufacturing villages established during the rebuilding continued in active use, their alterations as telling as their original forms. The extant houses, barns, and fields serve as a means of reconstituting unwritten definitions of convenience and beauty, definitions not found in the prescriptive literature of the time. They allow the researcher to observe the connections between landscape, economics, and society. They force us to remember that, even as the mill sites became manufacturing villages and the small towns became cities, rural culture dominated the first half of the nineteenth century. American culture for this period cannot be understood if viewed from an urban perspective, as exciting as the developments in the growing cities were.[12]

The creators and critics of the improved rural landscape of the early republic did not see eye to eye because they viewed the farmscape from widely divergent perspectives. For the reformers the countryside was the source of national virtue where urban ways should never intrude. For the farmers the country was where they lived and worked—the site of their aspirations and achievements, their source of income and sustenance.

Without the combination of written documents and material culture, the interplay of improvement and classicism in early-nineteenth-century life remains obscured. On the one hand we have the contradictory picture created by the improvers and reformers of farmers as disorderly, backward upstarts and of yeomen as the very foundation of cultivated society, the Cincinnati of the new republic. On the other hand are the classically detailed but newly efficient rural residences of farmers striving not for georgic existence, but rather to keep pace with the modern world. Both the written and the built are incompletely understood if we ignore either the abstract or material foundation. The improvers were not merely nostalgic for a lost age, they believed a new golden age was imminent. The builders were not merely applying pretty ornament, they were establishing property owners' places in the new nation.

To say that such things as economic opportunity, improved farming practices, or shifts in production caused the changes in the New England countryside is to give only a partial accounting. At the root of these actions was a change in attitude, an improving mentality that allowed and encouraged the physical change. Understanding the changes people made in their surroundings requires understanding some of the mental reordering that occurred, as revealed through their words as well as through their buildings. Just as the rules governing acceptable personal behavior changed with the growth of the nineteenth-century temperance movement, for example, so too did the rules governing acceptable building practice change as people adopted new notions of beauty and convenience. Improvement, whether spiritual or physical, of the individual, the farmscape, or the nation, was only a means to an end. The end was to demonstrate a sound moral character. In adopting these new standards New England's rural inhabitants revealed their personal virtue as clearly as if they had signed a temperance pledge. Events, then, do not determine substantive cultural changes. Rather it is underlying notions, attitudes or perceptions of the world that determine change. To paraphrase Henry Glassie, the material manifestations of change are not the real change; the real change occurs in the ideas of which a culture is composed, in the rules of its competence.[13] The physical improvements, refinements even, that we see in the post-Revolutionary landscape are not evidence of a culture smitten with gentility or aristocracy, but with the ideals of democracy or republicanism. Beauty and culture did not belong to the gentry and did not represent attempts to emulate the aristocracy, but rather to usurp them. Self-improvement was a civic duty, the key to the survival of the republic. The improved landscape would demonstrate that the middling sort had become key players in defining and maintaining the new nation.

Reformers and Improvers

In October 1819, Josiah Quincy addressed the crowd at the Massachusetts Agricultural Society's Brighton Cattle Show. With an oratorical brilliance seldom, if ever, matched among the ranks of agricultural improvers, Quincy touched on every issue dear to New England's early-nineteenth-century agriculturalists and rural reformers. Farmers, to whom Quincy dedicated his comments, he described as "men, who are the chief strength, support, and column of our political society, and who stand to the other orders of the state, in the same relation, which the shaft bears to the pillar; in respect of whom, all other arts, trades, professions, are but ornamental work; the cornice, the frieze, and the Corinthian capital."[1] Quincy, a member of the Massachusetts Society for the Promotion of Agriculture (MSPA) for sixteen years, could count himself as among those conducting both "ornamental work" and the more essential task of farming. An avid agriculturalist who published the results of his scientific farm experiments in the *Massachusetts Agricultural Repository and Journal,* Quincy had also served for eight years in the United States Congress as representative from Massachusetts, and would go on to serve as Boston's mayor from 1824 to 1829, and as the president of Harvard College from 1829 to 1846. A man of both political and intellectual bent, he applied himself to an issue of national concern—the physical and moral condition of American farms and those who owned them, taking the Massachusetts countryside as his point of departure.

The pillars, or shafts in Quincy's analogy, of society Quincy knew as men with "great farms and small pecuniary resources; men, who are esteemed more for their land, than for their money; more for their good sense than for their land; and more for their virtue than for either." Yet Quincy feared for the average yeoman's small pecuniary resources, for his good sense, and for his virtue as he surveyed the countryside. Imploring his audience not to "let the sound, practical, good sense of the country be misled, by the false taste and false pride of the city," he directed their attention to the farmhouse, the very symbol of rural taste and sound judgment. The sight he beheld disheartened him, for there on the home lot stood

> a building thirty, or forty, feet square, two, or two and a half, stories high, four rooms on a floor, with an immeasurable length of outbuilding behind. . . . for years the house will not be wholly glazed; or if glazed, not clapboarded; or, if clapboarded, not finished; the destined portico is never put up; the destined front step is never put down; and the ragged clapboards, on each side of the front door, there they stand, . . . and the 'best room,' as it is called in the original plan of the mansion, there it stands, the lumber room of the family, for half a century . . . full of old iron and old leather; the stuffing of decayed saddles; the ragged relics of torn bed quilts; and the orts [*sic*] and ends of twenty generations of corn cobs.[2]

Slovenly farming practices discouraged him, but extravagant houses positively frightened him. Evidently, only the domestic aspect of the great rural transformation disconcerted Quincy. Large new barns and rural milling and manufacturing represented rural prosperity, and hence national strength, but unusually large houses could mean only that vice and luxury had insinuated themselves into the countryside.

Quincy's speech encapsulated issues of major concern to social and political leaders of the early republic, particularly the issues of status and power in an industrializing and urbanizing, but still predominantly agricultural and rural society. Did economic and political power lie in the country or the city, in New England or the rapidly developing west? How could the nation judge whether or not it was headed in the right direction, whether or not this republican experiment would succeed? Quincy and other members of the relatively recently formed agricultural societies promoted the idea that husbandry, central to both the moral and economic strength of the state, held the key to the answers. When Josiah Quincy surveyed the rural landscape of the early republic, he saw both economic potential and moral corruption. The potential lay in the land. At Brighton, he advised farmers to maintain neat, comfortable, and orderly yards and fields, to heed their manure piles, and to mind their fences. A farm, even a small New England farm, properly maintained would recompense its owner more than adequately, but only if he could avoid the lure of the corrupting influence of luxury.

In his Brighton speech Quincy drew on a rhetorical tradition of ancient lineage, and on artistic conventions of more recent origins that colored contemporary elite views of what rural areas, as the heart of a modern republic's virtue, should look like.[3] The classical rhetorical tradition derived from English Renaissance adaptations of Virgil's georgic poems. Anthony Low has argued that in the seventeenth century England experienced what he calls a georgic revolution that paved the way for the agricultural revolution of the eighteenth. The georgic mode—a celebration of agricultural labor and the heroic quality of farming—combined with scientific advances and religious reform to lead to the acceptance of the virtues of labor by the noble and genteel classes, which had hitherto relished, and been defined by, their leisure.[4] Quincy inherited his reverence for, and idealization of, those who labored in the earth, directly from the agricultural improvers of the eighteenth and nineteenth centuries who continued to promote farming as the key to a nation's material and spiritual well-being. In essence, by using classical metaphors the reform-minded gentry could justify the maintenance of the status quo—that is, a region of small, independent farmers who, in spite of their independence, marked their inferior status in the types of homes they built.

To rural improvers and reformers like Quincy the appearance of the landscape reflected a nation's moral soundness. They, like their British counterparts, adhered to the notion that cleanliness, order, and simplicity—visible manifestations of economy—indicated the presence of a virtuous and hardworking household. English architect Richard Elsam's declaration in 1816 that "whatever has a tendency to improve the general appearance of the country, has likewise a tendency to improve the general morals, manners, and condition of the people," found adherents among American rural reformers. Where in England these efforts at rural improvement aimed to influence the "labouring classes of society," in the United States such improved landscapes and homes would harbor generations of upstanding citizens suited to a new republic.[5] If the homes of farmers failed to meet accepted standards of beauty, cleanliness, and economy, did that not mean that the very foundations of the new republic were threatened? With the disruptions of the Revolution past, the reformers incorporated into their own country estates English principles of landscape design and scientific principles of farmstead layout, which by their example they expected to spread, on a less grand scale, to lesser farmers. But farmhouses, a breed apart from the mansions of country estates, needed to look like farmhouses, the reformers' vision for which descended from the seventeenth-century picturesque landscapes of Claude Lorrain, not the villas of Palladio.[6] In Lorrain's paintings, the reformers found the pictorial realization of the rural ideal.

As had happened subsequent to Edmund Spencer's resurrection of the literary georgic form at the end of the sixteenth century, Lorrain's pastorals were further conventionalized and idealized over the next two centuries. The result in the new United States was that the stereotypical farmhouse in American art and literature celebrated Jeffersonian republican values while hiding the realities of rural life (fig. 2). That farmhouse eschewed fashionable trim, it became a timeless, plain form—something with colonial allusions, perhaps a saltbox or gambrel roof, but otherwise an image out of time.[7] By propounding an associationist aesthetic theory, in which certain styles were associated with and deemed appropriate for particular uses or contexts, reformers could move from an absolute view of beauty to a relative one, thus distinguishing between appropriate, and therefore beautiful, forms for a farmer's house, and their own rural retreats. Quincy and his improving and reforming cohorts concerned themselves, to some extent, with the actual productivity of farms and farmers. But they could not divorce those practical ends from the issues of public and private virtue, of which the farmscape gave material evidence. Economic gain could not be achieved at a moral loss, for then the republic itself was lost. For the rural reformers, the two-story-with-ell house cropping up all over rural

Fig. 2   Ralph Wheelock's farm, c. 1822. In this farmscape all is in perfect order. The hard work of haying appears effortless, laborers and haystacks alike are as neatly aligned as the buildings in the distance, and the hayfield is as immaculate as the dooryard visible just beyond the fence line. Ralph Wheelock's Farm. Gift of Edgar William and Bernice Chrysler Garbisch. Photograph © 2002 Board of Trustees, National Gallery of Art, Washington, D.C.

New England was out of place on an average working farm for economic, philosophical, and aesthetic reasons. To them it symbolized decay.

Quincy's farmhouse description offered at Brighton exaggerated the characteristics of an increasingly common rural dwelling form. Avery Ward's house in Sutton illustrates the type. In 1825 Ward, then twenty-nine years old, built a house and a barn on a half-acre of land one-and-a-half miles east of Sutton center on the road to Boston. A teamster soon to turn farmer, Ward had just moved to Sutton with his wife of eleven years, Jane Maynard, and their two children. The Wards built a fashionable house for themselves, identical in plan to several others already standing in town and, like them, embellished with classical detail. The five-bay dwelling stood two stories tall and had a hipped roof. The main house was only one room deep, but a single-story, one-room rear ell, accessible from the front right room, provided additional space. The house plan would have been familiar to Sutton's earliest inhabitants (fig. 3). The centrally located front door opened into a lobby entry with a dogleg stair. To the left was the formal parlor, to the right a less formal room. Unlike the most common pre-Revolution houses, however, the chimney stack was not located directly behind the entry lobby. Instead, in this modern, single-pile version of the hall-parlor plan, chimney stacks rose on the rear wall of each room. A small room occupied the space behind the entry.

The Wards' builder provided their house with modern finish details. Aside from the overall form of the house, the front door made the most visible statement of style. Narrow, fluted pilasters; sidelights; and another set of larger, plain pilasters, supported a slatted fanlight beneath a broad, simply molded entablature. Inside, narrow, double-beaded molding popular in Sutton in the 1810s and 1820s surrounded cupboards, doors, and windows. Chair rails and baseboards were simple, but boasted classically inspired profiles, recalling entablatures and bases of the ancient architectural orders.

By 1825 the form and details of the house that the Wards built were nearly formulaic. Although reminiscent of older building traditions in many of its details, the house synthesized old and new in a new, modern, way. Agricultural improvers and rural reformers denounced these classically detailed, two-story-and-ell houses, benign enough to us, as a threat to the moral fiber of the nation. The Wards' house, and others like it throughout New England, flew in the face of all that the reformers knew to be right and true.

In a society as dependent on oral transmission of information as early-nineteenth-century New England, all had access to the symbolism of classical references, even those who could not or did not read. Although by 1820 rural

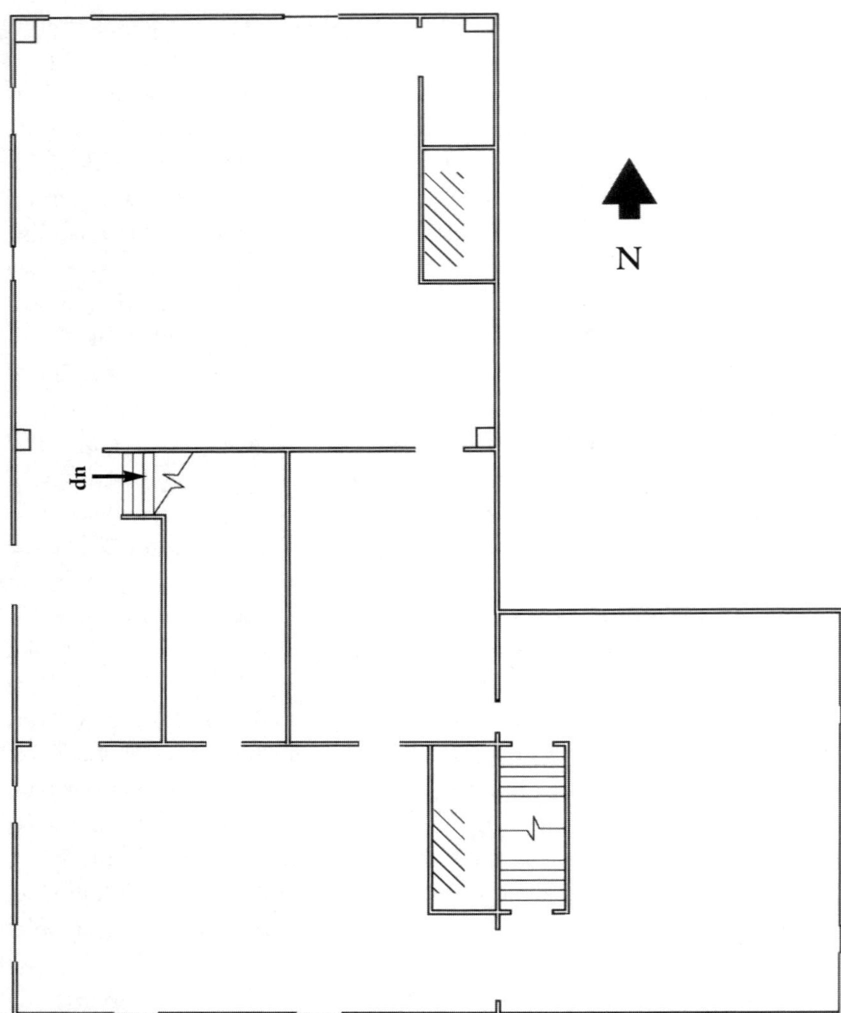

Fig. 3 | Avery Ward house, plan. Drawing by the author.

New Englanders were gaining access to increasing numbers of publications and could communicate through the post as well, face-to-face communication remained an important means of transferring information throughout the nineteenth century.[8] But a good many rural folk did read, and they would have been confronted fairly regularly with writings such as the letter that appeared in the *Massachusetts Yeoman* beginning, "I am the son of a farmer, a

Sutton farmer, and am as satisfied with my pedigree as though I could trace it back to the Caesars." Describing his viewing of a plowing match and the pleasure of seeing fellow townsmen among the victors, the correspondent wrote, "I would say to them, 'Persevere in your agricultural enterprise. . . . Let field and fence, and orchard, yard and farm-house tell the passing traveler that the spirit of a Cincinnatus lingers among your charming landscapes.'" Finding inspiration in the plowing match he proposed "that it be designated by a name that shall sound more *classical* than the one it has received. For plough-ing match I would substitute *Agrarian games*. . . . there is an obvious analogy between the ploughing sports and the ancient Greek games." He signed his letter "Georgicus."[9] Through such language rhetoricians imbued everyday activities with a higher meaning. To the agricultural improvers and rural reformers these were not mere farmers pitting the strength of their animals against each other; they were republicans tending the earth that the nation might thrive.[10]

We see in Georgicus's comments the tendency for improvers to celebrate farmers and farming as direct links to the virtues of the classical past. Yet the homage paid agrarian pursuits in the late eighteenth and early nineteenth centuries was hard won and not universally bestowed. With the spawning of interest in scientific agricultural improvement in America in the mid-eighteenth century, farming started to gain respectability. Its practitioners, barring gentle-men farmers who were honorable by definition, gained respectability by asso-ciation as long as they also demonstrated frugality and industry. Beginning with Jared Eliot's mid-eighteenth-century writings, the rhetoric of American agricultural improvers and rural reformers took shape around a classically inspired theme of agriculture as the basis of a nation's wealth, and the ancient republican- and Christian-inspired view of farmers as the pillars of morality on which a nation's virtue rested.

Commencing in 1747, Jared Eliot of Killingworth, Connecticut, a minis-ter and doctor by training and farmer by avocation, set out through a series of essays to assist his fellow countrymen in the reclamation of their soil and in the elevation of that most worthy occupation, husbandry. In Eliot's pioneering work on American husbandry we see many of the same themes later utilized by agriculturalists of the new republic. In his preface to the essays Eliot took a distinctly ministerial tone: "Certainly the Cultivation of the Earth affords the most useful Philosophy, opens to us a glorious scene and discovery of the Wisdom and Power of the Creator and Governor of the World. It is what has employed Men of all Rank and Orders, from the Prince to the Peasant."[11]

In the fourth essay Eliot commented that the pleasure of observing the life-giving spring fields far exceeded the gaudy shows and fleeting joys of urban existence. He extolled husbandry and navigation together in his fifth essay as "the true source of natural or real Wealth," but in the end husbandry came out ahead of all sources of wealth, "Without Husbandry, even Navigation cannot be carried on. . . . Husbandry then is a Subject of great Importance without which all Commerce and Communication must come to an End, all social Advantages cease, Comfort and earthly Pleasure be no more."[12] It stands to reason that with improvements in husbandry would come improvements in the rural built environment. Indeed, the Reverend James Bannister took up an old argument when he linked the rise of architecture, as opposed to mere building, to the establishment and growth of an agricultural economy: "Architecture, properly so called, owes its rise to agriculture."[13] While referring to what was perceived as historical truth, it was no coincidence that the debate over rural architecture in New England accompanied a sea change in the agricultural economy of that region.

Eliot's acknowledged classical sources on husbandry were Cato's *De Agricultura* and Virgil.[14] European Renaissance writers revived the works of Cato and Virgil along with Hesiod, Xenophon, Varro, and Columella which, taken together, established the place of agriculture in politics and society by concluding that agriculture was the supplier of all needs and the source of happiness, the country was the seat of honor and virtue, and the city was the repository of all manner of vice.[15]

The language of rural virtue that had taken root in English thought and literature more than a century earlier blossomed on American soil during the eighteenth century. By the late eighteenth century a cohort of statesmen, improvers, and philosophers—those embedded in an elite culture of thought and letters—viewed the connection between rural life and virtue as unquestionable truth. Their classical and biblical sources told them that virtue was inherent in the pursuit of husbandry. Only through that occupation could one fulfill the biblical injunction to make the land and beasts productive, thereby achieving not only agricultural improvement, but also moral improvement. Through husbandry one could achieve the independence of spirit and means essential to live free in a republican nation, thus demonstrating personal virtue of the sort promoted by the classical writers. A nation thus composed of free and independent agrarians would strengthen the nation's independence and economy, and consequently promote public virtue.

Gentleman farmers formed agricultural societies in Pennsylvania in 1785 and in Massachusetts in 1792 not merely to promote scientific agriculture, but also to promote their vision of public and private virtue. Historian Tamara Thornton has concluded that the gentlemen who belonged to the Massachusetts Society for the Promotion of Agriculture (MSPA) viewed their memberships as public demonstrations of virtue.[16] As an organization intended to benefit others at the expense of its members, the agricultural society served the same role as service in public office had in the colonies. In fulfillment of the social contract that afforded them prestige, deference, and positions of power, the gentry provided the general populace with instruction and the benefit of their example. Unfortunately, while the gentry attempted to promote their version of the social contract, the working farmers were up in arms. State and federal economic policies that harmed people still enmeshed in traditional economies culminated in Shays' Rebellion in Massachusetts in 1786–87, and in the Whiskey Rebellion in western Pennsylvania in 1794. The unrest in New England did not cease with the settlement of those disputes, but continued in Maine (at that time the northern Massachusetts territory) into the first decade of the nineteenth century as settlers fought attempts by absentee proprietors to throw them off lands to which both sides laid claim.[17]

The notions of agriculture as the source of all wealth and farmers as the virtuous souls who labored to produce that wealth served both as political rhetorical device and as a means of judging the success or failure of the republican experiment begun in 1776. The Reverend Nathan Fiske of Brookfield, Massachusetts, a successful market town in the mid- to late eighteenth century, took up these themes in a series of essays published in the 1780s and 1790s.[18] In the midst of farmers' growing distress, he admonished his readers that national prosperity and happiness should be the object of everyone. "Every person . . . in the community," he wrote, "has it in his power, and should have it in his wish, and in his practice, to contribute something to the advancement of the glory of his country by being honest and faithful, industrious and peaceable."[19] Fiske did not intend these words as mere inspirational verbiage, but as a scolding for those unpatriotic troublemakers who questioned those in power, and who failed to submit quietly to their burdens.

Fiske believed strongly in voluntary associations and in the duty of individuals to improve themselves. He noted in a 1790 address to the Minervean Society of Brookfield that "Improvement . . . is the business of man.—Ignorance and indolence are equally a disgrace to a rational creature."[20] He found the efforts of his fellow citizens to establish academies and societies commendable, noting that they marked the time as "an inquisitive and improving era."[21] Fiske commended most highly the efforts of certain gentlemen "of the first character" to pursue careers in agriculture. He observed that agriculture "has been degraded by the manner in which, and by the persons by whom, it has been carried on." With the involvement of citizens of upper rank, however, farming had become an "honorable employment." This had been achieved by placing mere brute strength "under the direction of reason and judgment, of thought and contrivance, of philosophy and system." Under the watchful eyes of these gentlemen farmers, agriculture rose "to the importance of a science." As practiced by a scientific elite, farming was a credit to the nation. As practiced by the common farmer the cultivation of the earth had been degraded to "a low and slovenly state," and only discredited its practitioner and the nation.[22]

A conscientious reformer, Fiske went beyond condemnation of average farmers to offer inspirational tales of reform. In one essay he portrayed himself as a farmer, "a middling liver," and addressed his essay "To the Neighbor." He described himself as a fellow who had changed from one jealous of all gentle folk to one content with his lot: "I considered, too, that though a farmer's life was laborious; yet in all labor there is profit, and health and honor too, . . . and our great *Washington* who was better than all the kings that are now in the world was a farmer. . . . [I]f ever I meant to deserve the character of a good man, I must be submissive to providence, and contented with my lot; . . . if ever I intended to be a useful man I must continue to be industrious and faithful in my calling."[23] For Fiske and fellow conservative elite improvers virtue for common citizens lay in maintaining the status quo. If they took pride in their station, honor would come to them through their honest labor. If they continued to follow the advice of their betters, common farmers could help to realize the success of the first republic to come into existence since ancient times. If not, they threatened to destroy the entire noble experiment with their selfishness.

In the wake of intense partisan conflicts in the late eighteenth and early nineteenth centuries, the traditional leadership not only found itself minus its old base of support from the common folk, but also found itself suffering from internal divisions. Seeking to mend the fabric of genteel society that had been nearly destroyed in the partisan wrangling, the gentry reunited under the guise of voluntary associations, particularly agricultural societies. Historian John Brooke, in his work on Worcester County, has found that the tumultuous politics of the early republic sundered the unity of that county's elite class, resulting in the loss of a considerable number of seats in the Massachusetts Assembly, and thereby compromising their political influence and power. Federalists and Republicans in Worcester County worked together to establish the American Antiquarian Society (1812) and the Worcester Agricultural Society (1818), and gentlemen of both party affiliations served together as officers and directors. These societies permitted at least a pretext of unity among the county elite, while ostensibly serving a greater good.[24] The fact that the gentry viewed farming as a metaphor for patriotism, virtue, and frugality, and used their new voluntary associations as a means of seeking common ground can be seen quite clearly in General David Humphreys's address to Connecticut's agricultural society in 1816:

> Let it not be believed that the love of country is extinct. Let us seek this point of re-union, around which we may rally. In the cause of Agriculture there can be nothing to disunite us. . . . A well-instructed, honest, hardy and laborious yeomanry, in cherishing his common interest, will pursue the best measures for preserving their republican character and moral institutions. . . . [M]ethinks I see the Fury of Party extinguish her baleful torch, drop her hissing snakes, and listen with charmed attention, whilst we thus celebrate the rites of Agriculture, at the shrine of Patriotism.[25]

Early-nineteenth-century addresses to agricultural societies are replete with staunch avowals of the virtuous character of husbandmen and the virtues of husbandry. These men spoke both figuratively and literally. They knew full well that their agrarian vision had a political dimension, but political life and personal life were deeply intertwined. Lewis Bigelow, a builder and contractor, delivered an oration before the Worcester Agricultural Society in 1820 that typified the genre: "Whether we regard the profession of agriculture for its antiquity, as the great and almost only source of human sustenance, or for its moral and social advantages, the subject is entitled to a preeminent rank among the pursuits of a civilized and enlightened people. . . . it is the cultivation of the soil which is the great source and basis of national wealth, power and grandeur."[26]

Whereas Bigelow chose to emphasize the Roman classical and subsequently Jeffersonian theme of national greatness through agricultural pursuits, Isaac Goodwin four years later trumpeted the biblical and georgic qualities of husbandry—personal virtue through agriculture—to the same organization. With the revivals of the Second Great Awakening and the surge in urban populations as his backdrop, Goodwin declared, "The cultivation of the earth is the employment destined to man by his Creator. It is the occupation of all others best fitted to promote his health, by alternate rest and labour; to preserve his virtue, by withdrawing him from the contagion of the more busy world, and to advance his civilization, by calling him away from the scenes of violence incident to roaming life, to the cultivation of the soft arts of peace."[27] Goodwin, a lawyer and justice of the peace, had joined the Worcester Agricultural Society in 1818, the year it was established. A member of Worcester County's elite, residing at various times in Sterling and Worcester, Goodwin was active in several of Worcester's cultural and financial institutions.[28] Not having to make his living from the land, he could afford to view agriculture from a metaphorical distance, and to extol an agrarian vision completely at odds with the realities of the marketplace.

When Henry Coleman addressed the agricultural society of Hampshire, Franklin and Hampden counties in 1833, farming and farmers retained their preeminent position, although he alluded to the increasingly popular view of commerce and manufacturing as valuable elements in the elevation of American citizens' well-being. Befitting his training as a minister, he employed biblical imagery of man subduing the earth. The farmer, he said, caused the earth to "impart sustenance and power, health and happiness to the countless multitudes, who hang upon her breast and are dependent on her bounty." In keeping with centuries of reliance on classical texts he concluded that, "Agriculture is a great subject. The first of the arts, it may derive aid from them all. The foundation of human subsistence, comfort, and enjoyment, the origin of all wealth, and the basis of commerce and manufactures, it deserves the profound attention of enlightened and philanthropic minds."[29]

To the reformers, simply being a farmer did not entitle one to agrarian laurels. You had to farm scientifically, and your aim had to be, not material wealth, but self-improvement and national greatness, from which personal wealth would flow. The Reverend Enos Hitchcock had set the standard in 1793 when he published the story of Mr. Charles Worthy. In Mr. Worthy the rural reformers found precisely the sort of farmer the young nation required. The story's subtitle sums up the required attributes: "or the History of Mr. Charles Worthy. Who from being a poor Orphan, rose, through various Scenes of Distress and Misfortune, to Wealth and Eminence, by *Industry, Economy and Good Conduct*." Inspired by the example of Mr. Smith, "an extensive landholder, and very respectable farmer," Worthy settled on the frontier. He did not, however, forget the amenities of civilization. He raised his children properly and built a comfortable house for his family. Farmer Worthy's house was both reward for and material manifestation of his industry, economy and good conduct. Although he did not specify its height,

Hitchcock implied, through the absence of a garret, that the dwelling stood one or one-and-a-half stories high.[30]

Here was a farm family, respected by all who knew them, who lived well yet simply. Their cultivated lives and lands inspired a city couple to reformulate their opinion of farm life, which they found ultimately preferable to their own. This rural utopia never existed and never would, but reformers and improvers believed it could. With enough manure, sweat and economy, and in common folk a taste for the beauties of nature over the artificial ornaments created by uneducated craftsmen, the agrarian vision would be fulfilled. The way to personal and national virtue lay in the cultivation of the earth, and the evidence of that virtue lay in the appearance of the landscape.[31] An anonymous author expressed the concept in an 1813 review of Archibald Alison's *Essays on the Nature and Principles of Taste.* Noting that the ancient Greeks used the same word for the beautiful and the good, the author concluded that in order for a man to possess taste, he had to be a good man. All of his "judgments and feelings of beauty" would be affected by the extent of his "moral depravity."[32] It stood to reason that tasteful farmscapes revealed virtuous farmers, and slovenly ones bad character.

For Timothy Dwight, as for Enos Hitchcock, thrifty, thriving farmers stood as symbols of the promise of the new nation. Dwight, farmer, minister, and president of Yale, repeatedly held up those who cultivated the land as exemplars of the social discipline that required healthful and moral living. The people of Brookfield, Massachusetts, Dwight noted, "principally farmers," had always "borne an honorable character for industry, sobriety, and sound morals."[33] Similarly, the farmers of Northborough, who apparently accounted for the entire population, were "sober, industrious, and thrifty," and constituted one of the wealthiest congregations in Worcester County.[34] Dwight often based his assessment of local character on the physical appearance of the place. He saw sound morals and prosperity in the handsome buildings and well-ordered farms that he observed on his travels throughout the Northeast. In New Haven he pointed out the beauty and healthfulness of the arrangement of a "considerable proportion of the houses," with front courtyards ornamented with trees and shrubs, and rear yards filled with "fruit trees, flowers, and culinary vegetables."[35] In the upstanding community of Princeton in the hills of Worcester County "[t]he houses of the inhabitants and the appearance of their farms are sufficient indications of prosperity; and the people are distinguished for industry, sobriety, and sound morals."[36] Dwight equates neatness and order with beauty, and beauty with virtue throughout his observations.

In his published travels Dwight expressed the belief that in the cultivation of his farm, a New England farmer gratified "his reason, his taste, and his hopes."[37] In so saying, Dwight advocated the right and responsibility of the average farmer to cultivate his mind and his judgment as well as his soil. Those who exercised this right owned prosperous and well-ordered farms that served as outward manifestations of inner characteristics, and would no doubt go far in ensuring the success of the republican experiment, not necessarily through political participation or activism, as Richard Bushman has pointed out in his analysis of Dwight's epic poem *Greenfield Hill,* but simply through their own 'sound morals' and financial stability. This combination would breed satisfaction with the status quo.[38]

The popular agricultural press that arose in New England in the 1820s also proclaimed the links between physical appearance and virtue. Articles and books from the agricultural press extolled the virtues of clean landscapes and explained the moral repercussions of sloppy ones. Samuel Denny wrote in his 1824 treatise on agriculture that any breach in the economy of cleanliness was "a breach in the character and property of everyone who allows it."[39] The *New England Farmer* proclaimed in 1827, in near-hysterical tones, that a neglected dooryard signaled a slovenly farmer, slovenly wife, and slovenly house. In 1829, in a tone worthy of the environmental determinism of late-nineteenth-century progressives, the editors made the implications of dirt and disorder even more explicit, "Neatness and order, whether on a farm, in a barn, a dwelling house, or in a man's dress and manner, are as indispensable to competence, comfort, and happiness as the sun is to day light. Neatness is necessary to health as well as to respectability. The want of it in cultivation and domestic economy, is extravagant as well as disgraceful. A slovenly husbandman or housekeeper is on the high road to ruin."[40] In order to be viewed as even moderately respectable, rural residents had to make themselves and their surroundings conform to new standards of order and neatness. Anyone who ignored these new expectations posed a threat, not only to themselves, but to civil and moral order.

In 1823 the *New England Farmer* drew a clear correlation between neatness and happiness on the one hand, and dirt and misery on the other, and to that added a public dimension.

There is something so pleasing in the appearance of neatness and cleanliness about a dwelling house, that even a stranger . . . cannot help being prepossessed with a favorable opinion of those within. He passes along with the idea fixed in his mind of prosperity and happiness presiding within those walls. How different the sensation felt on viewing a contrary scene,—a house dismal and dirty, the doors and walls surrounded and bespattered with filth of all denominations, and fragments of broken dishes and dirty dairy utensils scattered in all directions impress on his mind the idea of misery and mismanagement.[41]

Cleanliness and tidiness not only offered visual cues to a family's financial standing and personal character, they also affected those who witnessed them. They had the power to elevate their practitioners and passersby. Self-improvement, in other words, led directly to public benefits, a worthy goal for a classically minded republican.

To achieve the most public benefit from his display of farm and home, the farmer had to present not only a clean and tidy appearance to the world, but a tasteful one as well. A writer in the *Christian Spectator* regarded the man who "surrounds his dwelling with objects of rural taste, or who even plants a single shade tree by the roadside, as a public benefactor." The "taste and intelligence" of such an individual, or family, showed clearly in "the external air of their dwelling." An act as simple as beautifying a rural homestead had the power, he declared, "to affect our social and moral feelings."[42]

The belief in the ability to affect public virtue through private virtue has numerous origins, but the interconnection between ethics and aesthetics may be traced back to the third Earl of Shaftesbury's 1711 publication, *Characteristics of Man, Manners, Opinions, Times.*[43] Shaftesbury argued that objects that aroused feelings of pleasure were beautiful and good. The popularization of the theories of the beautiful, the sublime, and the picturesque in the second half of the eighteenth century in England also contributed to the belief that objects had the power to arouse various emotions through associative memory, and thereby raise the beholder to new heights of moral sensibility, to affect "social and moral feelings" as the *Christian Spectator* stated. All architectural writers of the nineteenth century dealt with the subject. In 1834 William Dunlap noted that, "the effect of domestic architecture upon moral feelings and character of mankind, renders it a subject not to be disregarded by us."[44] He then cited Timothy Dwight's *Travels* as evidence of the equivalence of virtue and right building. A. J. Downing seems also to have taken a cue from Dwight when he wrote in 1849, "show us a Massachusetts village adorned by its avenues of elms, and made tasteful by the affection of its inhabitants, and you also place before us the fact, that it is there where order, good character, and virtuous deportment most of all adorn the lives and daily conduct of its people."[45] William Ranlett, in his 1847 *The Architect* concluded that "[t]here is so intimate a connection between taste and morals, aesthetics and Christianity, that they . . . mutually modify each other: hence whatever serves to cultivate the taste of the community, will be likely to improve their morals."[46] To rural reformers a beautiful, tasteful, clean, and tidy countryside bespoke a morally upstanding citizenry. The reformers demanded that these characteristics be most evident on farms, the source and yardstick of a nation's moral fiber and material wealth.

If the state of a farmer's homestead and fields bore evidence of his character, and if his status as an independent yeoman depended on his simple, but good, taste and frugality, then, rural reformers concluded, the ideal farmstead consisted of tidy, economical (i.e., small) buildings on just enough acreage to supply a competence. As with most matters related to rural life, the reformers and the farmers no doubt differed in their definition of what constituted a competence. The early-nineteenth-century farm family studied by Daniel Vickers found its competence in "propertied independence," and the ability to participate in the market or not, as they chose, in order to sustain that independence.[47] Timothy Dwight's farmers, praised in *Greenfield Hill,* also sought propertied independence, but with a significant difference. Profit and the market played no role in the Reverend Dwight's 1794 idealization of a rural New England village. Envisioning farmers strictly as moral beings, Dwight and others promoted the rejection of the market, and even of political participation, which they viewed as antithetical to rural virtue.[48] A true inheritor of the spirit of Cincinnatus would reject participation in politics as unseemly, and instead devote himself to his agricultural holdings, to be called from his plow and his rural pursuits only when his country needed him. Farmers did participate in the market, however, and that participation resulted in enough profit or credit to allow the farmer to improve his holdings. When the middling farmer presumed to build two-story, classical dwellings, improvers and reformers feared the loss of rural taste, and hence rural virtue. Whether on the frontier in the 1790s or in the long-settled New England communities in the 1820s, economy guided reformers, and economy precluded the construction of large houses and indulgence in store-bought items. Without frugality, household independence, which ensured national political independence, was doomed.

New England's post-Revolution agricultural improvers believed that the conservation of time, space, and materials all went hand-in-hand with one another and with the success of the republic. They advocated cultivating small farms, contending that too many acres lay in waste when a farmer of average means owned much land. A man who cultivated a small farm embodied virtue, for he wasted nothing. In a true Jeffersonian spirit, an 1829 article cautioned that, "a firm and independent spirit is better nourished among that rank of men by whom small farms are cultivated. They are actuated by the same spirit. . . . their simple virtues will give its character to a country, and uphold in the hour of danger, the rights and liberties of all."[49] Farmers with not more than fifty acres could "rear large and respectable families, pay all their debts and taxes promptly, and live independently, well-clothed, and comfortably housed" because they wasted no time. The writer reminded his readers that "Economy is wealth, and system affords ease."[50] These respectable small farmers, using their time wisely, had no need to hurry except at harvest time. Even during bad weather or long dark winter nights they occupied themselves profitably with making brooms or shoes, or following trades such as coopering or tailoring.

At a time when fifty acres was close to the norm for much of New England (fifty-eight in Sutton), these writers advocated small farms as much as a means of maintaining the status quo as for reasons of economy. New England was suffering mightily as a result of out-migration and the booming western economy. Reformers argued that if people made the most of what they had, all things—a competence, comfort, ease, and certainly a better life than that available on the frontier—could be theirs. Such farmers upheld the republican principles on which the still-new nation had been founded, and would ensure New England's continued political influence.

Imbued with this agrarian republican vision, reformers could only take a dim view of the evidently overly costly two-story-with-ell farmhouse that seemed to be everywhere as the post-revolutionary generation rebuilt the countryside. "It is well known," wrote New York architect Minard Lafever in 1820, "that in common, the Farm House is too large, and consequently often not well furnished, and perhaps unfinished, which arises from the expenses being greater than the direct proceeds of the farm on which it is erected. . . ." Lafever urged designers to plan with an eye to "frugality, convenience, and neatness, in a plain style," and, perhaps recalling the dominant house forms of the pre-revolutionary generation, "never advise the farmer to build more than one full story besides the basement, and a garret. . . ."[51]

Agricultural journals of the 1820s and 1830s took farmers to task for their assault on virtue, and urged them to build housing more suited to the countryside. The farmer who heeded the principles of economy, they declared, lived in a small house. From a mild admonition in 1823 counseling farmers not to begin by building a costly house unless they had a good deal of capital, the

New England Farmer progressed to more damning tones.[52] In 1825 the journal printed a condemnation of rural building practice that singled out farmers as the worst culprits.

> The practice which Farmers have unadvisedly fallen into of late, in building too large houses, besides impoverishing them, is at variance with correct taste. . . . There is nothing connected with a farm, considered either as an object of taste or economy, that is more pleasing or delightful than a small house. . . . The wish to be thought of more importance than we really are, and the notion that this importance will be estimated from the spacious mansions in which we may reside, is too prevalent among every class of society; but in no one is the consequence more prejudicial, or its influence more deeply felt, than in the agricultural community. There are few dwelling houses in the country two stories in height, which do not contain at least two rooms that seldom, if ever, are appropriated for any other use than the solemnization of a marriage or obsequies for the dead.[53]

The writer concluded that had the farmer built a smaller house he would have been "encircled by many sincere friends, with a competency of this world's goods to make life comfortable, imparting joy and content to a virtuous and happy family." As the source of the nation's virtue, rural areas had to be preserved from the corrupting influences of urban extravagances and unnecessary displays of wealth. The common farmer could make a public statement of virtue, of his taste and economy and his continued role as patriarch, only in a small dwelling.

As the Massachusetts Society for the Promotion of Agriculture turned its attention to horticulture in the late 1820s, the image of the proper farmer's house developed into something akin to an idealized English peasant's cottage.[54] The picturesque English cottage itself had emerged as a stock image in late-eighteenth-century England just as enclosure radically altered that countryside, and threatened the very existence of the thing idealized. More than memorializing a lost way of life, English landscape painters turned the peasant's cottage into something timeless, turned the countryside into georgic or pastoral existence. It turned that which had been abandoned and left to ruin by the agricultural revolution into something attractive, something to be valued.[55] The appeal of this picturesque imagery to a New England gentry rapidly losing its political hold on an industrializing countryside is not surprising. Of course, in the United States, no one suggested that this picturesque way of life was what had been lost; rather they suggested it as the thing to which New England farmers should aspire. More than one writer compared the virtues of the English countryside and its convenient and beautiful cottages festooned with "the woodbine and honeysuckle," to the ostentation of the New England farmer who rears "a huge exterior, whose construction exhausts his resources, and leaves neither disposition or resources to complete the interior." Such a one ignored the natural ornaments "richer than those which the chissel [*sic*] of the sculptor has ever worked" which might grace his abode. Instead, the slovenly garden "seems to call out shame on the listlessness which neglects its beauties."[56] In 1833 "J. S. M." of the Horticultural Society sent a letter to the *New England Farmer* in which he commented on the absence of rural taste evident throughout New England. The farmhouses of the region, he wrote, lacked the picturesque gardens of English cottages. These might be provided if the farmer spent his money on "the embellishment of houses and farms" instead of on spirits.[57] No hope remained that virtuous republicans occupied the transformed New England countryside. It seemed evident to the reformers that taste, public virtue and private morality had all fled in the face of selfish indulgence.

And who were these people who had destroyed the republican vision of rural reformers? They were themselves improvers with an equally compelling vision of material prosperity and personal virtue. They had every reason to believe that the new home lots they fashioned would pass to their progeny, and often undertook the work with the future beneficiaries. They did not build only for themselves, or as the *New England Farmer* insisted, "to be thought of more importance than we really are." They built in a manner suited to their station and in accordance with new standards of decency—in accordance, that is, with the rules of taste and economy. Although some builders or improvers of two-story-with-ell houses no doubt overextended themselves, the evidence from Sutton suggests that most were well placed to undertake such a building campaign. More broadly, the presence of securities in rural Massachusetts inventories beginning in 1778 suggests that there was money in the countryside to invest or spend. Country folk did not necessarily burden themselves with excessive debt in their building campaigns.[58]

This profile of Sutton's improvers comes from a sample of seventeen properties built or improved between 1790 and 1840. Twenty-two men participated directly in the building campaigns on those properties.[59] Although most of the owners of the new form of house did not style themselves gentlemen, they were nevertheless among the wealthiest and most securely established individuals in town. Hailing from families that had come to Sutton in the first wave of white settlement or married into those families, bound to the community by an extensive safety net of kinfolk, these people did, indeed, obtain "a competency of this world's goods." Land records referred to only three of these twenty-two men as "gentleman" or "esquire." Nine were styled "yeoman," and the remaining ten held such occupations as tanner, housewright, millwright, lawyer, and cashier.

Indications of occupation or status alert us to the fact that no one group was more prone to build in this manner than another, but mask other characteristics of these local improvers. The two gentlemen, for example, were both working farmers, and neither accumulated as much land as merchant Lazarus LeBaron. The wealthiest man among them, LeBaron was called only "merchant," but his occupations included tavern-keeping on a grand scale and farming on extensive holdings. LeBaron died in 1828 with more than 250 acres to his name. The two millwrights also farmed and built houses. Joshua Armsby Jr., designated a housewright in legal records, served at four sessions of the state legislature and held local office for many years in the 1820s. The self-styled yeomen died with extensive collections of carpentry and blacksmith tools in their barns and sheds. Formally identified with one occupation, informally these men wore many hats.

Property ownership came with age in New England, if it came at all. The average age at the time of building improvement for this group was forty-two, with the range being twenty-four to seventy-two years old.[60] Because father and son frequently undertook improvements jointly, however, an average age is less useful in establishing a profile of these improvers than is their stage of life. The non-exceptional case of Bartholomew and Simon Hutchinson, father and son, serves as illustration.

In January of 1806 Bartholomew Hutchinson, then sixty-five, deeded one undivided half of all his land and buildings to Simon, his youngest son, who still lived on the old homestead with his father and stepmother. Simon married Vandalinda Morse the following November, at age twenty-seven. It seems likely that in the intervening months, in preparation for the creation of a new household, Simon and his father added the one-and-a-half-story ell to the east gable end of the eighteenth-century farmhouse. They thus left the long shed roof and rear second-floor half-story of the old building intact, and presented a modern big house–little house façade to the street.

All of the builders in this group were either already married when they undertook the building campaigns or married within two years of the undertaking. Some of them built starter homes; some who had been married anywhere from six to twenty-five years, built new houses or added to older ones to accommodate two households and changing housekeeping practices. Our improvers' ages ranged widely, but they undertook their building campaigns either after years of labor or with the backing of an already well-established family member.

The extent and value of property holdings among this group of men testifies to their financial security. Nine of them owned property in town in 1798, the year of the federal direct tax census. Five of that group had inherited their lands from their fathers. Six of the nine passed it on to their sons. In 1798 their holdings averaged 132 acres while the town average was 87 acres. Their home lots with houses, barns, and occasional outbuildings, were worth $678, more than twice the town average of $323.[61] We can measure wealth again in 1830, with similar results. The improvers' acreage averaged 113 acres, nearly twice the town-wide average of 58 acres. They held real estate, including home lots with buildings, worth $2,563 on average, while the average for the whole town was $1,474.[62]

These twenty-two men could count more than extensive property holdings among their privileges. Seventeen of them were born in Sutton to families that had arrived in town around or before 1750. Another, Peter Sibley, was born in the neighboring town of Uxbridge, but was related to the Sibleys who had settled in Sutton by 1731. Two others married women whose families had been in town since before 1730. Only two seem to have had no connection to the town prior to the Revolution.

Persistence of families in one place for two or three generations generally produces sizeable kinship networks. Even counting only the family names of husband and wife, the improvers were related to an extensive number of households.[63] Half of them had reached their majority by 1798. In that year each was related to approximately eleven households. For the eleven who came of age and married after 1798 the number of related households fell off slightly to just below ten in 1830.[64] Their continued residence in Sutton and their extended families had much to do with their success, and with their ability to manifest that success in their building activities.

Jonathan Dudley Jr. is one who seems to have benefited from his family connections, at least for a while. In 1826, a year after his marriage to Sarah Torrey, Dudley, named as merchant in the deed, bought a two-story, single-pile house with rear ell, a barn, and a shed in the village of West Sutton. His account book of 1828 indicates that he was a storekeeper in that village. These material remains suggest that in his late twenties Dudley had attained his competence and the means for holding onto it. Tax records suggest otherwise.

By 1830 Dudley owned no real estate and his only personal taxable property consisted of a chaise worth fifty dollars without even a horse to pull it. His father on the other hand, a cooper by trade, was taxed for one-and-a-half houses, two-and-a-half barns, a cider mill, 170 acres of land, a chaise and horse, four oxen, nine cows, and other livestock. Between 1835 and 1841 Dudley Jr. acquired two acres, a cow, and a hog, but still possessed no buildings of his own. He may have been living in one of the two houses that his father and younger brother owned jointly. By 1845 he owned a house and barn and eleven acres but no livestock. We can probably attribute Dudley's ability to stay in town to family assistance. His death in 1847 at age 48 or 49, brought on by a diseased liver and dropsy, implies that Jonathan Jr. was a hard drinker and suggests a reason for his inability to establish himself despite his well-off kin.[65]

All told, twelve of the seventeen properties passed between close family members. Most transactions were between fathers and sons or sons-in-law, although in one case the property passed to a niece. The families that retained their property for more than one generation held that property for an average of 118 years, thus affording a stable base for at least one household in each generation. New England settlers throughout the colonial era and into the nineteenth century courted this kind of stability, that is, the ability to pass lands to successive generations and to settle family members in close proximity. Nathaniel Putnam, having inherited his farm from his father Cornelius in 1761, attempted to oversee the family estate even from the grave. He willed his estate in 1812 to his son Moses but stipulated that on Moses's death the property was to be divided equally among his fifteen grandsons, a partition that would have strained the ability of the farm to support those who owned it.[66] The possibility of attaining a competence for self and family such as Cornelius Putnam had done in Sutton in the 1720s spurred the settlement of frontier areas at the end of the eighteenth century as it had at the beginning.[67] The two-story landscape that mushroomed in central Massachusetts in the post-Revolution era can be seen as a celebration of the realization of this ideal. Just as successful residents of the older towns to the east had done in the eighteenth century, these well-established middling and prosperous sorts resorted to two-story dwellings when circumstances permitted it.

The agriculturalists accused rural folk of overbuilding, of living in houses where whole rooms were given over to junk or used only for rites of passage such as marriages and funerals. In addition, however, to providing spaces for the processing and storage of numerous farm products and home manufactures, these dwellings often accommodated two households. The building boom in Sutton between 1800 and 1830 coincides with a slight lowering of the number of households per dwelling, from nearly two households to 1.5 households per residence, but the statistics indicate that dual-family households remained common well into the century.[68] These successful improvers did not simply pass their property on to the next generation when they died; they resided with the younger generation, often selling an undivided interest in the property to their heirs with stipulations for their own maintenance as long as they lived.

As common as it may have been, the accommodation of multiple households under one roof required a certain amount of spatial orchestration, to which the houses and family documents testify. In 1806 Bartholomew Hutchinson sold an undivided half of all of his property to his newly married son Simon, who brought his bride to live at his father's house. The old house consisted of a two-story, center-chimney, hall-parlor house with rear lean-to. The addition of a second household prompted the construction of new spaces. Instead of raising the rear slope of the lean-to to create new second-story rooms in the main block of the house, a common eighteenth-century practice, the Hutchinsons built a side ell. The story-and-a-half ell was asymmetrically fenestrated with one window to the left of the door and three to the right. Eyebrow windows did not align with first floor windows. The chimney stack stood off-center, to the left of the door.[69] The scale of the ell indicates that it could have housed either the new family or service activities displaced from the main house in order to accommodate properly two separate households.

When Malachi Marble died in 1810 his widow continued to occupy the two front rooms of the house and a chamber. Their son Ezra continued to live in the rear of the house, and possibly one chamber, with his wife and two young children. The two households shared the cellar, garret, well room, and cheese chamber. We also know from Enoch Stockwell's codicil to his will that his daughter Abigail and son-in-law Palmer Harback had "come to reside with me in my old age and at my request." While it is not entirely clear how the two families shared the elder Stockwells' ell house (built around 1806), the dower set off to Enoch's widow, Nancy, suggests that the older couple occupied all or part of the main block of the house. Nancy received the west part of the big house, which consisted of the parlor, the second-floor chamber, the garret over, and the cellar under that same end. She also took possession of the entry, the stairs to the cellar, chamber, and attic, and had a "right to bake in the oven in the kitchen in the remaining part of said house."[70]

All told, of the seventeen dwellings under consideration here, seven housed two related households in the early nineteenth century, with as many as fourteen people under one roof.[71] In another case an unmarried adult relative resided with the family, ultimately inheriting the property and sharing it with an unrelated household. An 1830 letter from one of Worcester's leading ladies, Mrs. Stephen Salisbury, to her son Stephen Jr. attests to the common nature of this house-sharing arrangement among all classes, "'I will tell you what would please me. It is that you would be married and live with me till you could at your leisure build and furnish such a house as you would like. You should have the drawing rooms entirely to yourself and I can assure you they are most pleasant rooms to live in.'"[72] Evidently, these local improvers not only had not built beyond their financial means, they continued to use the new spaces intensively, just as they had for generations.

The rural reformers' political agenda and aesthetic proclivities did not mesh with the locals' economic realities and cultural expectations. In refusing to defer to the opinions of their "betters," farmers attacked one of the presumed components of classical republicanism—that the virtue of "the many" derived in part from their deference to, or respect for, the few. On the other hand, country ideology in England redefined virtue in the eighteenth century to consist of independence—an independence that assured that an individual could dedicate himself to the *res publica* with no regard for "other men and their social structures."[73] Farmers presented a conundrum for New England's rural reformers, for they were both the cultivators of the earth, with all that that appellation implied, and commercial beings. Farmers, enmeshed in commercial markets and attuned to the effects of government fiscal policy on their economic well-being, embodied the "inveterate opposition between the agrarian man of independent virtue and the professional man of government and commerce."[74]

Local improvers and absent reformers shared an interest in transforming the rural landscape, but had different motivations for doing so. Far from being concerned with fulfilling reformers' vision of what a prosperous republican countryside looked like, farmers sought to secure their places in the new economy and new political order. One way to do that was to alter their workspaces (domestic, agricultural, and artisanal) to efficiently accommodate new work and social processes. In so doing, they turned to very different sources than the reformers had drawn on, to determine the public face and internal arrangements of their rebuilt homesteads.

Chapter 2

Beauty
The Architect's Ideal

While reformers based their notions of proper rural domiciles on perceptions of political and social hierarchy and on a picturesque aesthetic, American architects proposed a landscape based on the absolute beauty of classical forms, and the natural beauty of objects designed to fit their purpose, that is, objects designed for convenience. In getting down to the business of literally building a new republic, the fine art of architecture was the object of popular public discussion and debate. All agreed on the importance of the built environment because of its role as indicator of public and private virtue, national and individual prosperity. Many feared that the taste of increasingly well-off Americans would not keep up with their ability to purchase status symbols hitherto available only to a very elite group. As the *Massachusetts Magazine* noted in 1789, "The passage is very short from elegance to luxury. Ionick [*sic*] and Corinthian columns are soon succeeded by gilt cornices, inlaid floors, and petty ornaments, which shew rather the wealth than the taste of the possessor."[1] Luxury was to be avoided at all costs in a simple agrarian republic. But how could Americans' taste keep pace with their pocketbooks? Architects, master builders, farmer-artisans, and farm wives all entered into the exchange, promoting or creating variations on the classical theme, working to compose their own versions of beauty and convenience, to imagine and construct tasteful and useful landscapes. None seemed to agree with the rural reformers that the transformation they participated in boded moral and economic degeneracy. Nor did they agree with the fashionable world that the countryside should consist of picturesque settings replete with happy peasants.

Over the course of the eighteenth century classicism became synonymous with beauty, and beauty with virtue. To architectural theorists of the Enlightenment the new style, dubbed the "true style," contained the timeless quality of truth that had given Greek architecture its power and enabled it to persist through the ages. Mid-century European theorists like Abbé Laugier and J. J. Winckelmann maintained that classical architecture had reached its apex among the Greeks. In England, too, the idea gained popular acceptance through the works of the likes of theorist and designer Robert Morris. In his *Select Architecture* Morris praised Greek accomplishments over Roman noting that architecture "was in Perfection in Greece long before the building of Rome."[2] Citizens of the new republic of the United States encountered the same sentiments in their own popular publications. The *Massachusetts Magazine* published the Reverend James Bannister's thoughts on the subject in 1789. Bannister maintained that in Greece "we see the elegant arts cultivated to that high degree as to leave succeeding ages only the humble task of imitating what they could never equal."[3]

When the muses arrived on the shores of America, and their arrival seemed imminent to mid-eighteenth-century American colonists, they would come bearing the truth and beauty of what was called Greek architecture, but which in reality often drew on ancient Roman sources, either directly or by way of English Palladianism. In 1760 Ezra Stiles, minister to the Second Congregational Church in Newport, Rhode Island, asserting the artistic equivalent of the political autonomy that colonists were beginning to yearn for and demand, preached on the auspicious future of the arts and sciences in the colonies and concluded that "in a few years we shall have . . . Painting, Sculpture, Statuary, but first of all the greek Architecture in considerable perfection among us."[4] "Greek" architecture in this sense was a generic term for the more archaeologically correct use of the ancient orders, whether as used by the Greeks themselves or the Greek-inspired Romans. Stiles saw evidence of the progress of the arts on American shores in the works of the often Roman-inspired Peter Harrison. He cited Harrison's Redwood Library of 1748 among his reasons for accepting the call to serve as minister in Newport.[5] With the arts firmly ensconced on American shores, the colonies would have one less area in which they needed to depend on England.

The "true" or "modern" style, still without a uniform label, dominated architectural theory and design at the time that the American colonies gained their independence from England. Richard Elsam, an English architect, argued for its use in rural situations in his 1803 publication *An Essay on Rural Architecture.*

Responding to James Malton's advocacy of the picturesque, he objected that the irregular plans presented by Malton were "suitable for the peasant and farmer, who require no other guide in the construction of their habitations than the examples before them." The picturesqueness of those cottages arose from age, situation and climate, not from purposeful effect. The "great Architect of the universe" had Himself employed uniformity and symmetry throughout the animal world, and Elsam's designs followed suit. He recommended that the peasants continue to devise their own plans, but insisted that persons "of more refined taste and discernment" required "country houses in the modern elegant style."[6] With the picturesque being touted as well-suited to peasant dwellings, what self-respecting American farm family would wish to present itself in such a subservient role? While rural reformers may have found this to be enticing imagery, American farmers did not. They turned, not surprisingly, to the "modern" style associated with taste and discernment.

Architectural classicism, pejoratively dubbed neoclassicism in the mid-1800s, permeated American academic and vernacular building as architects, pattern book authors, and master builders sought to improve the new nation's architecture and to create a peculiarly American style in the process.[7] America, the next logical abode of the muses of art and science in their natural progression from east to west, needed to demonstrate its preeminent cultural position through its adaptation of the true style to its buildings. Monuments to classical principles appeared early on, in such works as Thomas Jefferson's 1785 Virginia Capitol and Benjamin Henry Latrobe's 1819 Bank of the United States, but those were only the most visible results of a far broader cultural phenomenon. While those great public projects took shape, Americans turned to builders and publications to guide them in the use of this modern style. On the shoulders of the architectural handbook publishers and the working architects rested the awesome responsibility of demonstrating the success of the American political experiment through its architectural accomplishments.

The era of rebuilding in rural New England coincided with the careers of Charles Bulfinch, Samuel McIntire, William Strickland and Benjamin Latrobe, and with a riot of newly published popular handbooks, including the works of Asher Benjamin and Owen Biddle. Classified as the Federal, Adamesque, or neoclassical era by architectural historians, the extensive nature of this rebuilding has often been commented on, and is beginning to be analyzed beyond the works of the above-mentioned handful of architects. All along the eastern seaboard builders constructed two-story houses with symmetrical façades, fitted out with simply framed windows and slightly more elaborate doors. Urban or rural, architect- or builder-contrived, wall surfaces were plain, and planar, barely marred by the windows.[8] In New England, the reading public encountered numerous descriptions of buildings that measured up to the ideal, such as that of Bulfinch's New Stone Church in the December 31, 1814, edition of the *Boston Spectator.* The author noted that here the architect had united "the massive simplicity of the Grecian temple, with the conveniences of a christian church." The finished church stood as a monument to Bulfinch's "taste and science," but also as evidence of a purer taste that "banish[ed] super-fluous ornament" and achieved its effects through "correct proportion and the richness of the material."[9]

All of this work was embedded in the international neoclassical architecture movement, which in turn was part of the Enlightenment's search for a new golden age modeled on classical precedent.[10] A completely rationalized architecture that harmonized with nature, based on scientifically understood natural principles, would symbolize the steps then being taken to advance the human race.[11] In the United States, as elsewhere, neoclassicism was not merely a fashionable mode in which to build architecture or furniture, nor simply a backdrop to daily activities or events of state. Classicism imbued all aspects of intellectual discourse—whether that discourse took the form of political debate or agricultural theorizing—and was as available to the educated masses as to the economic, political, or religious elite.[12] When used in architecture, a classical vocabulary evoked Roman stoicism, Greek rationality, and, in general, the republican virtues of the ancient world, as well as, to some, absolute beauty. While the fashionable world sought to transform the countryside into something reminiscent of the great seventeenth-century landscape painterly ideal, rural builders and their clients sought a style suited to a dynamic and democratic republic.

Neoclassicism took hold in the work of rural New England builders as quickly as in the work of the region's most celebrated practitioners of the style, Charles Bulfinch and Samuel McIntire. Both Bulfinch and McIntire moved only gradually from colonial and English precedents to a full realization of the neoclassical ideal. In their early work, for example, they used the old-fashioned high-hipped roof with balustrade surmounting it. In later work they lowered the roof pitch and moved the balustrade to the eave line.[13] Bulfinch, whether constrained by budgets, tradition or his own inclination, modified the neo-classical tenets that he had absorbed during his European Grand Tour of 1785–87 for his Boston clients.[14] The country estate that Bulfinch built for Mrs. Swan in Dorchester conformed to local preference in many details.

Second-story dummy windows disguised Bulfinch's neoclassically inspired en suite rooms, which would have been more properly highlighted by a dome. He sheathed the exterior walls with clapboards rather than the smoother masonry-like stucco or painted brick.

Just as Samuel McIntire's decorative work evolved over a thirty-year period from sturdy to delicate to austere as he gradually adopted neoclassical ideals, so too did rural builders move erratically from the robust and heavy proportions and ornaments of the eighteenth century to the more delicate and attenuated proportions and ornaments of the Federal era. In some cases they consulted the same architectural handbooks that Bulfinch used, including William Pain's best-selling *The Practical Builder* of 1792, which popularized the neoclassical style. In other cases they had direct access to the masterful work of Bulfinch and McIntire, either through their own peregrinations, or those of the masters. Bulfinch, for example, achieved one of his finest architectural moments in the rural town of Lancaster in Worcester County. In his Lancaster Meetinghouse of 1815–17 Bulfinch realized the neoclassical ideal of chasteness and geometrical purity. And yet, even there a local master builder, Thomas Hearsey, supervised and carried out the actual construction. Bulfinch, having provided the plans, never visited the site.[15] While working on such projects or observing the completed work provided rural builders with direct access to cutting-edge design, they also could consult the numerous publications of Bulfinch's avid pupil, Asher Benjamin, among others.

The widespread distribution and ballooning numbers of American architectural handbooks beginning in the early nineteenth century contributed significantly, as their authors hoped, to the transformation of the built environment. Just as architectural works published in England in the early eighteenth century had made academic architecture accessible to increasing numbers of builders and patrons on both sides of the Atlantic, so too did this spate of publications widen the audience for academic classicism still further.[16] Authors of these handbooks and pattern books believed that the new republic required a new set of architectural guidelines. Owen Biddle expressed his determination to contribute to the transformation of American architecture in his 1805 *Young Carpenter's Assistant,* "I can conceive of few objects of more consequence, in a new and improving country like our own, as it regards our health and convenience, or as it may gratify the fancy, than the proper construction and building of our houses."[17] For the first time in an American architectural handbook, Biddle presented the four classical orders with explanatory text, giving the reader the history and uses of each.[18] Proper design entailed the correct use and interpretation of the forms of antiquity. For Biddle, the attenuated classical orders popularized by Robert Adam in the 1760s in England constituted proper interpretation of the modern style.

Asher Benjamin, in his *American Builder's Companion* of the following year, rejected old interpretations of classical form more explicitly. After introducing his "new System of architecture" he wrote, "Old fashioned workmen who have for many years followed the footsteps of Palladio and Langley, will, no doubt, leave their old path with great reluctance." But Benjamin, having worked with Charles Bulfinch in Boston, was convinced that "a reform in some parts of the system of Architecture is loudly demanded." He based his new system on a lightening of heavy parts and the consequent reduction of expense in labor and materials. His interpretation of classical theory served not just the elite, but also Everyman: "We are well aware that the magnificent temples of ancient time still retain a degree of romantic grandeur, which would do honour to the present age . . . [but] a strict conformity to the orders of Architecture seems to be demanded in the construction of public buildings only, and others of immense magnitude."[19] This architectural system, which avoided the "massy size and the expense" of the more exact interpretations of the classical orders codified already fashionable practice. Like Biddle, Benjamin based his American architectural system on the internationally popular neoclassical proportions. He justified its use, however, by maintaining that this delicate classicism better suited American finances and "convenience." American architecture, then, whether designed by Bulfinch or by the scores of rural builders at whom Benjamin directed his books, was purposefully distinct from European. American builders, operating from a different set of assumptions and circumstances than their European or English counterparts, intended not to follow European precedent, but instead to follow classical precedent, to make the only proper architectural vocabulary their own.[20]

While presenting rural builders and patrons with current classical forms, builders' guides like Benjamin's and Biddle's also provided general rules, principles, and critiques of current building modes that allowed, even encouraged, interpretation of the classical orders and decorative detail by local builders and their clients. Beginning in 1811 with the publication of the second edition of Benjamin's *American Builder's Companion,* architectural handbooks included sections on the history of world architecture.[21] By doing so, Benjamin and his successors displayed their own command of the theory and principles of architecture, but demonstrating competence and proving one's suitability to practice and teach architecture were only part of the goal. They also provided the increasingly independent middle class with the tools needed to build their own cultural identity. In order for the classical vocabulary to have meaning, it had to be understood. The pattern book authors of the early republic era provided not only specific examples of the orders, but also their historical contexts and justification for modern interpretation. They knew that their audience would not be those who could afford to hire a Bulfinch or a Latrobe, but that vast middle rank of city and country dwellers that had been the leaders in consumption of material and artistic culture for much of the eighteenth century. Driven by a desire to create public expressions of taste, and therefore of morality, the middling rank took classicism, and its acknowledged inherent beauty, to heart. More broadly, the new dwellings demonstrated the type of enlightened knowledge, what one might call cosmopolitanism, required of a republic's citizenry if that republic is to succeed.[22]

Where some have seen a spread in urban culture in this sort of access to information and dissemination of ideas, we can read instead a new broad-based cultural expectation, not urban or rural, simultaneously experienced in city and country.[23] Perhaps this was particularly true in New England which contained on its seaboard six of the ten most populous cities in the United States in 1790,[24] and in its western reaches a wealthy merchant gentry with ties to major trade centers. The line between urban and rural culture had to be blurred in a region where the non-urban population had such easy access to urban areas, and the urban population to rural areas. It took Paul Revere only four hours to ride out to the hinterlands from Boston on April 18, 1775, albeit in a rush, suggesting fluid communication from center place to center place.[25]

Worcester, less populous even than Sutton to its south or Brookfield to its west, became home to a supposedly urban institution when the patriot printer Isaiah Thomas fled Boston in April 1775. Thomas published the first Worcester issue of the *Massachusetts Spy* on May 3, and the *Spy* remained a local institution until 1860.[26] With gentlemen and patriot leaders such as John Hancock, Samuel Adams, and Benjamin Franklin passing through Worcester during the war, and in the case of Franklin even stopping to assist Thomas with a repair to his presses, this non-urban community may not have recognized urban and non-urban culture, but might instead have distinguished between modern and not modern, or republican and non-republican. It is not too much of a stretch to suggest that since Boston's Radical Whigs had essentially enfranchised all men who held property, and some who did not, by taking the political debate to the very public forum of open town meetings, those men became emboldened enough to assert their new political power, their new social standing, in the way in which they built or rebuilt their houses. Not only did "the active engagement of common farmers and tradesmen profoundly [change] the character of public life," as Richard Brown asserts, but it also evidently profoundly affected the public presentation of self.[27] The point is, that new ideas may have been circulating too rapidly, and even emerging from such non-urban points as Worcester, for us to label certain cultural developments, such as notions of beauty and convenience or proper republican architecture, as urban. Elkins and McKitrick, in trying to explain the perceived lack of cultural accomplishment in the colonies, have pointed out that there was "no specific setting in place or time in which [politics, government, economy, intellect, art] could act upon each other."[28] Rather than supporting the idea that there was no cultural attainment, their argument suggests that the urban/rural dichotomy by which some have judged the presence or absence of culture is simply not adequate to that task, ignoring as it does period perceptions of center and culture.

David Jaffee has addressed the issue head-on in his discussions of village enlightenment in post-revolutionary New England. Numbers and location of printing presses, artisanal shops, and merchant manufacturers indicate a multitude of commercial and cultural centers, their existence made possible by the improvements in transportation and the subsequent improvements in communication and commerce. No longer tied to centers of trade in Connecticut, clockmakers, for example, moved to New Hampshire, and small center villages in the upper Connecticut River valley developed into major print centers. Cabinetmakers, chairmakers, and other artisans throughout rural New England took advantage of improved access to markets, materials, and pattern books to produce stylish goods for rural populations.[29] For a time, decentralized production of all manner of commodities put rural towns at the center of local and regional exchange systems in which ideas flowed as easily as goods. The result, as Jaffee has pointed out, was the toppling of "traditional cultural mediators" from their positions of power, a displacement that they fought on many fronts, including the architectural one.[30]

The slim lines of neoclassical architecture, of Benjamin's American system, appeared in the massing and ornament of Sutton buildings by the first decade of the nineteenth century. So early, in fact, that one suspects Benjamin was making a virtue of an already established fact—American rural buildings tended toward simplicity. By offering plans, ornament, and massing that complemented the established vernacular or to which the vernacular could be easily adapted, the "new system" of architecture had a better chance of being adopted.

The 1800–1806 single-pile Enoch Stockwell farmhouse is a case in point. Stockwell, a successful farmer and self-styled gentleman, bought or built a house suited to a man of his wealth and stature. Minimally ornamented on the exterior, the house evoked the new spirit in building with its narrow profile, simple cornice returns, and interior end chimneys. Elaboration of interior structural elements centered on the fireplaces in the parlor and kitchen. The builder finished the parlor fireplace, at the west end of the house, with a delicately molded and tiered mantel and an equally intricate firebox surround. The kitchen fireplace, at the opposite end of the house, was less formal, having fewer layers of molding, but like its counterpart in the best room, the moldings adhered to the attenuated proportions and delicate lines of the neoclassical vocabulary.

The simplicity of the style can be seen again in the early-nineteenth-century remodeling of the mid-eighteenth-century Harback family house (fig. 4). Around 1800 the owners of this house on Boston Road raised the rear lean-to to a full two stories. About ten years later they added a rear ell. When

Fig. 4 C. Harback house. The slight asymmetry evident in the front façade, in the chimney's location just to the front of the ridgeline, and in the side elevation are the result of an early-nineteenth-century remodeling of this eighteenth-century dwelling. Photograph by the author.

Thomas Harback house, cornice detail, c. 1812. Photograph by the author.

completed, the remodeled façade bore a distinct resemblance to the Stockwell's plain front. The cornice employed the simplest of moldings, calling to mind a Tuscan or Doric order, and the doorframe was barely elaborated. A simple molding constituted the door architrave, while a line of lights above the door and a barely projecting cornice suggested an entablature.

In the 1810s opening surrounds and entablatures became more elaborate, less subtle references to classical orders. The cornice of the Thomas Harback house (built around 1812) evoked the Ionic order in its degree of elaboration, although not in its detail (fig. 5). Its cyma recta was finished with punch work; beneath the fascia ran rope molding and dentils, the whole finally completed by a cyma reversa molding. Inside pilasters on pedestals framed a chamber fireplace, and a projecting mantel served as cornice (fig. 6). The Harbacks followed more customary practice in a second chamber, however, eschewing the more modern mantel in favor of raised panel doors to either side of the fireplace, and a raised panel above.

Fig. 6 Thomas Harback house, chamber fireplace. Photograph by the author.

The Deacon John Morse house, built around 1811, and the 1813 Salmon Burdon house incorporated all of the modern elements of domestic design. These single-pile structures with low-hipped roofs, paired rear or interior end chimneys, and rear ells completed their statements of modernity with classically detailed fenestration. Fanlights topped front doors, and pilasters and a full entablature surrounded them. Although by no means archaeologically correct, Morse's door with its modillions and ornamented frieze called to mind the Roman Doric order, while Burdon's more austere treatment was reminiscent of the simpler Tuscan (figs. 7, 8). Full entablatures consisting of a cornice with cyma recta, fascia, and cyma reversa; a frieze of metopes and triglyphs; and simple architrave crowned the Morse house windows, while those of the Burdon house were more simply finished with cyma recta and cyma reversa moldings.

To builders and architects, and presumably to those who had the structures built, properly proportioned and employed classical architectural motifs signaled good taste. Neither taste nor the classical vocabulary that signaled its presence belonged to any particular social class. Far from attempting, and failing, to emulate their social and economic superiors, these improvers had defined taste and morality, beauty and convenience for themselves. The

Fig. 7 Deacon John Morse house, front door, c. 1811. Photograph by the author.

building public agreed with the intimate connection between taste and morals made evident in the writings of Timothy Dwight, Enos Hitchcock, and the agricultural press. They declined, however, to adhere to the strict plainness advocated by the rural reformers, instead ornamenting their

Fig. 8 Salmon Burdon house, front door, 1813. Photograph by the author.

dwellings with classically inspired finish work, and thereby offering evidence of their good taste, sound morals, and prosperity. An essayist in the *American Journal of Science and Arts* in 1830 seemed to take the side of these improvers when he took up the issue of why the fine arts had received little encouragement in the United States. He observed that some people, even "persons of enlightened understanding and liberal views" feared that the cultivation of the fine arts would compromise "that simplicity of manners, and purity of morals, which must form both the basis and bulwark of a republic. . . ." He took issue with this view, insisting that the "fine arts are perfectly consonant with good morals, and, so far from being the handmaid of luxury and licentiousness, have always operated as a check on their extravagance." Where handsome architecture and inviting public places exist, residents will be happier, and less inclined to roam, he wrote. Domestic architecture, he believed, should be cheerful and convenient. In order to achieve cheerfulness, the builder must use one of the three ancient orders, of which he recommended the "Grecian Ionic." Convenience he left to the discretion of the occupant.[31] By this author's definition, rural improvers, with their classically inspired architectural ornament, played an important role in bringing the fine arts, and good morals, to the countryside.

In assessing farmers' houses rural reformers made the same mistake that many modern architectural and cultural historians have made. They judged the houses based on a set of standards not employed by the builders and residents of those houses. Elkins and McKitrick, for example, used mid-nineteenth-century and early-twentieth-century critics of American culture to assess the success or failure of the creation of an American Athens and, not surprisingly, concluded that "most of the country remained something of a [cultural] wasteland for years to come."[32] Such judgment is fine when it seeks to discern objective differences in practices. The cultural historian can determine much from examining the houses of wealthy rural merchants in comparison to their urban counterparts, for example. But one thing she cannot conclude is that one was objectively better than the other. When a judgment condemns one set of practices as slovenly, misguided, or deficient in comparison to another, it sets up a false dichotomy. Twentieth-century assessments of rural building practices all too often read like reincarnations of nineteenth-century reform literature, judging American building to be poor imitations of finer achievements elsewhere (in the city, in England).[33] Richard Bushman was no doubt correct when he concluded that "Personal cultivation and the presentation of self in a select company was a protean ideal with undefined boundaries, no real center, and far-reaching effects, but it is the key to understanding life in the great houses."[34] Alan Taylor has certainly demonstrated the point in his analysis of William Cooper, and the efforts that Cooper took to bring gentility to the frontier and to ensure that he would be considered among the ranks of the genteel.[35] The question is, however, what did great-house culture have to do with everyone else? Were the "deficiencies of American styles" attributable "as much to delays and imperfections in the transfer of craftsmen as to rusticity in taste," as Bushman asserts?[36] In order to reveal the relationship between American high-style and vernacular cultures, we must ask who perceived deficiencies in American architecture, and why? In Bushman's work, we get the impression that culture belonged to a particular class or rank of people, and that they defined culture for everyone. In fact, the culture of classicism permeated society, and was widely available in print, in material culture, and in the oral culture of the day. The occupants of the great houses certainly defined gentility for themselves and for anyone who cared to join their ranks. Their attempts to direct the rebuilding of the countryside reveal their assumption that they could define taste and gentility for those they believed to be beneath them. The aristocracy's show, however, could only be for those who spoke the same cultural tongue, and moved in the same social and cultural circles.[37]

Bushman also presented us with a vision of "culture being carried from the metropolis to the provinces in the late seventeenth century in the minds and hands of English craftsmen moved by the currents of supply and demand." But those craftsmen came from the provinces, and returned thence when they had completed apprenticeships, supposedly with London masters. It is in the periphery where Bushman discovers "a dozen important provincial clockmaking centers" by 1700.[38] The craftsmen who established those dozen clockmaking centers had to make quick work of obtaining urban apprenticeships and hustling back to the boondocks to establish thriving clockmaking centers. A top-down or center-periphery model does not work in something as complex as creation and transference of culture. Whether in London, Boston or Sutton, one would be hard-pressed to find "pure" examples of the architectural ideal. Bulfinch bowed to local preference; his assistants, including Benjamin, moved easily between rural and urban employment; McIntire needed time to refine his architectural detail. It did not matter that Bulfinch and McIntire lived and worked in two of the most important commercial centers of the early republic; their work evolved in response to local circumstances, not as a result of perceiving themselves as having fallen short.

By eschewing emulation theory or top-down models we can see the pervasiveness of classical culture in the early republic, and the way in which the middling sorts translated that vocabulary and turned it to their own uses. While some, indeed, may have wished to emulate the urban gentry, and be accepted into their ranks, surely others wished to challenge the old power structure and assert their own dignity and worth. The theory of social emulation works only if the class purportedly doing the emulating in some way admires the class it is emulating.[39] If, as John Brooke has argued so eloquently, southeastern Worcester County was a bastion of oppositional politics, electing its local gentry to office and supporting economic independence, it makes sense that their houses were not bids to enter a suspect gentry class, but rather to assert their own place in the political and economic landscape.[40] Whether acting as pre-Constitution anti-Federalists or post-Constitution Federalists, the pattern in southeastern Worcester County was local control—first in the form of opposition to external government powers, be they British or American, and then in the form of strong local churches and voluntary associations.

By the time Sutton and other Worcester County towns had lost their political and economic preeminence to Worcester in the 1830s, architectural pattern book authors and architectural critics had almost abandoned the search for a virtuous republican architecture reflective of national strength in favor of a search for a virtuous domestic architecture, reflective of family strength. Like the early national reformers, these advocates for architectural improvement, now coming from within the architectural community, espoused the picturesque. Henry R. Cleveland, in his 1836 review of James Gallier's *The American Builder's General Price Book and Estimates,* argued that there were two forms of domestic architecture—the Palace style and the Cottage style. The Palace style was regular, suited to large homes, and able to handle Grecian or Gothic ornament. The Cottage style, on the other hand, suited "all dwelling-houses, whose interior is fashioned less with regard to the rules of architecture, than the convenient arrangement of the interior." That is, the Cottage style, in Cleveland's view, was appropriate for everyone outside of the wealthiest rank.[41] Taking up the longstanding argument that beauty and convenience go hand-in-hand, Cleveland contended that such buildings "do not depend upon architectural ornaments for their beauty, so much as upon their obvious fitness for comfort and use; and their forms, so far from being necessarily regular, are often most picturesque and beautiful when least symmetrical." As Josiah Quincy had done earlier in the century, Cleveland castigated country builders for sacrificing interior comfort to exterior grandeur, and for ignoring the natural beauties of gardens in favor of the artificial attractions of columns.

The post-revolutionary generation of architects and builders had believed fervently in their ability to create an American style, and thereby secure the new nation's cultural and moral standing. They had also believed that this architectural revolution would rightly take place in the countryside, the home of the yeomanry, the nation's pillars of strength. With the passing of that revolutionary and republican zeal, with the rise of the importance of cities and the continued democratization of the electorate, this next generation saw only failure in those early attempts. As early as 1814 George Tucker had predicted that failure in an essay for *Port Folio*. Acknowledging the intrinsic beauty and utility, or convenience, of Grecian architecture, Tucker argued that habit had led Americans to prefer certain Grecian forms. Recognizing Greek temples as some of the most beautiful architectural creations on the earth, Americans believed that Greek forms would naturally impart beauty to their own buildings. But that force of habit had also prevented Americans from deviating from Greek rules of architecture, to the point where they had sacrificed their own buildings' utility, and resorted to slavish copying.[42] An American architecture suited to an independent republic had failed to materialize. Mr. Cleveland provided a blunt assessment: "The rules of Architecture are probably violated more frequently, in practice, than those of the other fine arts, and in no civilized country are they less regarded, than in the United States."[43] In 1843 Horatio Greenough continued the discussion, maintaining that the United States had never seriously applied itself to building, and that the nation had only copied, and copied badly, the Greek, Roman, and Gothic styles. Developing the connection between beauty and convenience, or utility, in an increasingly nuanced argument, Greenough insisted that the human eye instinctively recognized organic beauty, and that the beauty of form arose from the fulfillment of function.[44] Where the architects of the new republic believed, at least for a short time, that beauty was absolute, and so they knew that convenience would arrange itself in a regular, classical manner, these architects held no such tenets. The principles of the picturesque, of romantic associationism, had muddied the waters. While beauty continued to be tied to fitness or convenience, the terms were redefined.

With the redefinitions came the reassessments of rural architecture. Derided as monotonous, "destitute of beauty" or over-decorated, the classicism of the first three to four decades of the century bespoke all too blatantly the failure of the United States to live up to its potential.[45] For the more generous or diplomatic architectural reformers, farmers and farming became, not the direct source of national wealth, but "the great nursery of all the professions and the industrial arts of the country." The countryside, having ceased to be the hub of political and economic activity, its role having been usurped by the growing strength of small and large cities throughout the nation, became instead the locus of rejuvenation, the retreat to which the lawyers and merchants could repair to revive their spirits, in A. J. Downing's words, "to be regenerated in the primitive life and occupation of the race [of farmers]."[46]

Such a retreat, and such a status, required simplicity. Where the architects of the new republic had sought to dignify rural architecture, not finding much difference in the circumstances of rural and town inhabitants, these antebellum architects, like the rural reformers of days of yore, promoted plainness. "The farmer himself is a plain man," wrote Lewis F. Allen in 1853, "His structures, of every kind, should be plain, yet substantial, where substance is required."[47] For Allen, the Italian, rural Gothic, or English cottage style all served the purpose. Yet Allen did not go so far as to advocate the then-popular earth-tone colors, which he found too somber for his taste. Nor had Allen given in to the picturesque in the matter of form. While his rural architecture may have been adorned in simple elements derived from ostensibly picturesque styles, his plans were all quite Georgian in character. The smaller cottage boasted a traditional hall-and-parlor plan with center chimney, the largest farmhouse a double-pile, center-hall plan. Complete with ells, these venerable plans still served as the embodiment of convenience. But such a consideration of the interior workings of the farmhouse was a rare occurrence in this era of pattern book publications. In spite of the occasional reference to the republican virtues of the countryside, the place of farmers and rural industrialists, merchants and mechanics had been usurped in the popular imagination by urban centers of power. The command that these numerous center-place villages had had over the economy and politics of the eighteenth and early nineteenth centuries had slipped. The new generation could no longer discern the meaning inherent in the edifices of their rural predecessors.

The loss of that meaning is nowhere so well illustrated as it is in the Reverend N. H. Chamberlain's "Paper on New England Architecture," read before the New England Historic Genealogical Society in Boston in 1858. His assessment of the New England countryside and its architecture could not have been more different from Reverend Timothy Dwight's of a half-century earlier. He characterized the buildings of the small farmer as "small, unpainted, and stained a motley black by the atmosphere. . . ." The farmers' weed-choked and rubbish-strewn yards stood in sorry contrast to the natural wonders all around. In the villages he found houses of "no style whatsoever," except that since they all looked alike and were all equally wanting in artistic merit, they may be said to have been built in "the New-England style." He did allow that the New England house "as to plan and detail, belongs to the Grecian style of architecture," but only insofar as it does not use the Roman round arch or the Gothic pointed arch, preferring the straight lines of the Greeks. "You may see in the lines and window-finishings and mouldings of many a black, unaesthetic farm-house, inhabited by most unclassical people, traits of classicism in its architecture." That classicism he did not attribute to any virtuous quality of the inhabitants, but instead to its ease of construction and relatively low cost, and wondered to what degree "those monstrosities of an Anglicized classicalism," popular in the eighteenth century and still disfiguring London, had influenced the builders.[48]

Aside from the absurdity of using classical forms in the New England countryside, Chamberlain had another bone to pick with those who had left such a blight on the landscape, and even continued to build in a similar manner. These houses with "trim white walls or monotonous paper; the square, unrecessed, open rooms; the prim, unaesthetic furniture," left nothing to the poetic imagination. He longed for a "house of the olden times," with its irregular rooms and bare oak beams, its dark corners, and garret full of "the neglected historic paraphernalia of the family." The romance, if not the ubiquitousness, of spiders and dust-laden odds and ends would have escaped Reverend Hitchcock's Worthy family, as much as the improvers who transformed their houses and farms in search of both beauty and convenience.

To this long tradition of critical assessment, stretching from the rural reformers' contemporary critique to the antebellum disillusionment with the previous generation's architecture, can be attributed the loss in meaning and the cultural devaluation of these farmhouses. Too presumptuous for early republic reformers, not quaint enough for mid-century romantics, not old enough for late-nineteenth-century antiquarians, nor lavish enough for twentieth-century architectural historians, their architectural logic and significance evaded many who cast their eyes over the New England landscape. These critics missed the fact that over the course of the revolutionary era, the cultural ideal of domestic space changed for middling sorts as they adopted a new definition of beauty, as economies transformed and as utilitarian demands on that space changed. The architectural press, not the agricultural press, had played a significant role in the promotion of that cultural ideal and the subsequent change in the exterior appearance of much rural New England housing. But while the new farmhouses presented a modern face to the world, they also owed much to tradition. We will turn our attention next to that mix of the familiar and the new.

Convenience
The Farmhouse

Over the course of the eighteenth century Sutton grew into the second wealthiest and second most populous town in Worcester County. For three decades after the Revolution it held this position. To its north, Worcester, the county seat, outstripped all other towns in the county in population and wealth; while to its west, the former Massachusetts frontier experienced unprecedented growth. During this period of seeming stasis for Sutton, the town actually experienced a period of conspicuous rebuilding and reordering as the post-revolutionary generation modernized its farms, houses, and shops, and as a new era of manufacturing dawned throughout the Blackstone River valley. Home to many of the farmers to whom the reformers addressed their pleadings and scoldings, Sutton's architectural heritage suggests that the working farmers ignored the proffered advice, building large numbers of two-story houses with side or rear ells and restrained classical detailing. In rebuilding their townscapes in the first decades of the republic's existence, provincial New Englanders did not blindly copy or ignorantly modify the stylish creations of more professional architects or more urbane patrons. They, too, participated in the modern classical culture. Their houses incorporated what they viewed as the twin principles of modern building—beauty and convenience. Tradition, work patterns, and the architectural press encouraged rural builders and their patrons in this course of action.

The farmhouse that led reformers to fear for the survival of the republic seems innocuous enough to us today. Removed from its economic, cultural, and even physical context, it serves primarily as a quaint reminder of slower, quieter, pre-industrial days. But post-revolutionary New England was not slow, quiet, or pre-industrial. Rural housing served as the reformers' index to dramatic change in the countryside, and it can serve much the same function for us, a point of entree into a rural landscape that changed in nearly all aspects in the space of one generation. By looking more closely at these houses than the reformers did, we can discern precisely what changed and what did not, what the builders deemed immutable, and what had to give way to modern need or sensibility.

Neither classicism nor the supposedly wasteful and extravagant two-story house were new to the post-Revolution hinterland, but their rapid post-war proliferation was. Although single-story houses dominated the eighteenth-century Worcester County landscape, outnumbering two-story dwellings two to one, by the end of the century two-story houses comprised from one-third to one-half of the housing stock in Worcester County towns of similar age and rank to Sutton, making them a familiar, although far from ubiquitous, form. As Michael Steinitz and others have suggested, much of this two-story land-scape across Massachusetts may date to the mid-eighteenth century and may have resulted from improved agricultural practices. Places such as the eastern county of Middlesex and the Connecticut River valley in the west were pro-ducing grain surpluses by the 1770s, surpluses that might well have financed the mid-century rebuilding.[1] Nevertheless, it appears to have been a rebuild-ing restricted to the wealthiest of the traditional gentry, a group that would find itself with both political and economic challengers following the war.

Whether one or two stories, most of Worcester County's houses clustered around 600 and 1,000 square feet in plan.[2] Throughout the Massachusetts Bay Colony builders commonly arrayed that square footage in a version of the center-chimney, hall-parlor, lobby-entry plan, a house type that had been estab-lished in parts of southeastern England by the first decade of the seventeenth century.[3] Since the first decades of settlement, Massachusetts houses had grown from plans of one room with chimney and often a lean-to, to two rooms or more with a center chimney. All phases existed simultaneously in the colony, but individual houses often began as a piece of the single- or double-pile, center-chimney, hall-and-parlor form. Over half of the first-period houses that Abbott Lowell Cummings studied for his groundbreaking *Framed Houses of Massachu-setts Bay* grew to their center-chimney, two-story form over time.[4] In Sutton, the evidence for this common practice of building by accretion survives in at least five houses.[5]

The "half-houses," so-called here to distinguish them from the fully real-ized center-chimney houses that they frequently became, but known in some parts of New England as the "double house,"[6] appear to have been the colonial version of a starter home. Several Sutton homeplaces, built prior to 1760 as two-story, single-cell, end-chimney dwellings, grew to center-chimney, hall-parlor plans by 1780. The half-houses appeared at least throughout the seventeenth century in eastern Massachusetts towns and throughout the eighteenth century in Sutton. The evidence in Sutton suggests that individual stage of life and fortune, rather than the stage of community development, determined the choice of this house form. We would expect, nonetheless, to find fewer half-houses being constructed as housing stock increased, and as the land available for start-up ventures grew scarce.

Joseph Severy, a married weaver with three or four children, arrived in Sutton around 1728, only ten years after Anglo settlement, and established a farm northwest of the center of town. He built a two-story, saltbox half-house with an east-end chimney, and possibly a single-story lean-to at the west end, the only wall that was plank-framed. In 1732 Severy sold this property to newcomers from Salem—Nathaniel Hutchinson and his bride Joanna Conant. By the time he died in 1756, Hutchinson had expanded the single-cell house to the east so that it stood as a complete two-story, hall-parlor saltbox dwelling. At that stage the house measured over 1,100 square feet on plan.

On the other side of town Stephen Hall, a farmer and a contemporary of Hutchinson's, built and enlarged his house in a similar manner. In 1735, at age twenty-six, Hall received sixty-one acres of farmland from his father. Within the next ten years, he built a half-house similar to that on the Severy/Hutchinson farm. This initial structure contained approximately 600 square feet of space on the ground floor. The expansion to a center-chimney saltbox dwelling may have occurred as early as 1752, the year incorrectly assigned as its original construction date in the old Sutton history, but definitely had taken place by 1779, the year Stephen deeded the farmstead to his son. Hall's single-pile house with full-length rear lean-to fell just shy of 1,000 square feet on plan. With the roof raised and the back wall pushed out to create deeper rear rooms, the Halls' house occupied over 1,200 square feet of ground prior to the end of the century.[7]

At the end of the first generation of white settlement, the half-house remained an option for establishing a homeplace. As Nathaniel Hutchinson neared the end of his life, Dudley Chase, a twenty-five-year-old farmer and second-generation Sutton resident, started on his career as home- and farm-owner. In 1755, Chase purchased ninety-five acres from his father. Like his older counterparts, he built a two-story, single-cell house with end chimney for himself and his wife of two years. Chase, like Hutchinson, used plank wall construction on the non-chimney, gable-end wall. About ten years later either Chase or his successor expanded the house, making it a full hall-parlor, central-chimney dwelling, 816 square feet on plan.[8] All told, these homes that grew from half-house to full house over the course of the eighteenth century averaged 983 square feet in their final form, well within the bounds of the typical Worcester County house footprint of 1798.

Even in the post-revolutionary years the half-house form remained in use. An undated house in Sutton, measuring just over 550 square feet, survives in its original single-story, end-chimney configuration. Standing by 1788 when its owners plastered it and scratched the date above a door, it provides valuable evidence of the intensive use of space in the eighteenth century and into the nineteenth.[9] Only two structural bays wide, with the chimney stack occupying one of those bays, the plan consists of three separate rooms and an entry lobby on the ground floor (fig. 9). The staircase in the entry gave access to the cellar and the garret, both usable spaces. Daniel and Prudence Hatheway and their six children occupied the place in the early nineteenth century, followed by the Rufus and Azubah Fuller family, again with six children. The chimney stack and fireplaces are gone (although the foundation remains), but the massive hewn and sawn framing testifies to the desire of its occupants to ensure the longevity of the house. The builder framed the cellar with two large carefully hewed beams, into which he inserted square sawn joists.

The half-house was, of course, only one option available to Massachusetts colonists. Some chose to construct the full hall-parlor plan in a single building campaign. Such a house could still range from 600 square feet to over 1,000. In Sutton, a mid-eighteenth century, single-story, gambrel-roofed, center-chimney dwelling measuring 684 square feet on plan remains standing as the side ell of an early nineteenth-century farmhouse.[10] Stephen Waters's two-story, center-chimney, double-pile house (built around 1757) occupied nearly 1,100 square feet of ground when built.[11] When the federal government conducted its direct tax census in 1798, most houses in Sutton and throughout eastern and southeastern Massachusetts would have stood as some variation on this center-chimney, hall-parlor form.

In the first quarter of the eighteenth century, another house form featuring a center passage and bilateral symmetry gained popularity all along the eastern seaboard. Constructed in Sutton only rarely in the eighteenth century, this "new" form would strongly influence the rebuilding of the post-Revolution years, in spite of the disapproval of improvers such as architect Minard Lafever who warned designers of farm "cottages" against the use of the wasteful center

Fig. 9   Eighteenth-century "half house." The original chimney stack stood behind the front door
and the lobby entry. Photograph by the author.

hall.[12] The center passage plan is one of the hallmarks of what architectural
historians have labeled the Georgian house. Full Georgian dwellings are characterized on the exterior by bilaterally symmetrical façades, matched chimneys
disposed in a balanced arrangement, and a hipped or gambrel roof; and on the
interior by a two-room deep plan and the center hall.

Architectural historians J. Frederick Kelly and Fiske Kimball both commented on the appearance of the center-hall plan in New England in their
treatises of the 1920s. Fiske Kimball dated the initial arrival of the central-hall
plan in the colonies to the late seventeenth century, when it appeared in such
houses as the Peter Tufts house (built around 1680) in Medford, Massachusetts, and the Sergeant houses (built around 1676) and Foster Hutchinson house
(built around 1689) in Boston.[13] Kimball maintained that the seventeenth-
century examples were rare and that the form increased in popularity among
the gentry in the second quarter of the eighteenth century. Kelly, too, wrote
of and illustrated late-seventeenth- and early-eighteenth-century examples in
Connecticut, but also dated the popularization of the form to later in the
1700s, in Connecticut to the third quarter of the century.[14] More recently,
Kevin Sweeney and Ritchie Garrison have pinpointed more precisely the

arrival of the center-hall plan in the Connecticut River valley in western Massachusetts to the 1750s.[15]

Since the 1970s, when Henry Glassie and James Deetz published their works on Georgianization along the eastern seaboard of the United States, this phenomenon has received considerable attention among scholars of vernacular architecture.[16] By adopting or adapting the center-hall, double-pile form, gentry could separate public from private spaces, create rooms for specialized uses, separate themselves from their social inferiors, and practice the behaviors of polite society with their peers.[17] Although New England's elite employed the form increasingly throughout the eighteenth century, the center-hall plan remained rare in the region's hinterlands.[18] In Sutton it made an appearance in the post-1763 Malachi Marble house.

While many of his contemporaries built or added to two-story, center-chimney dwellings, Marble chose to build a story-and-a-half, center-passage house with interior end chimneys, evidently on the site of an earlier single-pile, center-chimney, hall-parlor house. On the ground floor, the house contained one room to either side of a center hall at the front of the house, and two or three rooms across the back. Early-nineteenth-century alterations have made it difficult to discern the original configuration of rooms at the back of the house. With its thirty-foot-wide base, its tall posts and steeply pitched roof, the structure provided enough space for three finished chamber rooms, one of them a cheese room, and a full stand-up attic.

Malachi was a man of some means. The 1798 direct tax census valued his house at $360, slightly above the town average of $323. His taxable property undervalued his total wealth. At the time of his death in 1810 his total estate was worth over $8,000, and was evidently debt-free.[19] This well-to-do second-generation Sutton farmer built a dwelling of just over 1,000 square feet on plan, thus remaining well within the common experience of his neighbors, as well as of Worcester County inhabitants in general. He set himself off, however, with his choice of a center-hall plan. This center passage provided the opportunity to display stature within the bounds of local propriety. Malachi's builder finished the walls of the passage with vertical hand-planed sheathing boards with quarter-round molding. The staircase, not one of the more common cramped, closed-in winder or dogleg stairs, rose in a gentle incline from the first to the second floor. The balustrade, however, provided a distinctly unmodern note, being composed of balusters and rail of seventeenth-century proportions.

In this interpretation of Georgian form, the Marbles combined forms of comparatively modern derivation with customary design. The resulting house read from inside and outside as both familiar and slightly different. Approaching the house along the road from the east it would have appeared to the visitor to be a taller, more generously scaled version of any of a number of contemporary one-story structures (fig. 10). Superficially more modest than its two-story counterparts, the interior end chimneys signaled a departure from usual practice. Inside, the balustrade provided a reference to past decorative practices, perhaps having been removed from the earlier house, while the spacious center passage departed sharply from the cramped lobby entries of even its largest center-chimney contemporaries.

It took the wealth and space needs of Lazarus LeBaron, merchant, tavernkeeper, and farmer, to achieve the full Georgian ideal. In 1792 LeBaron built a center-hall house on a grand scale in Sutton's town center. The two-story, double-pile house with hip-on-hip roof exceeded all other local houses in elegance and ostentation. With the main house block measuring thirty-six by forty-two feet on plan and the ell extending to the back of the building for fifty feet, the LeBaron house exceeded by at least 1,400 square feet the footprints of most Worcester County houses. Yet this house was only a larger,

Fig. 10   Marble house, northeast corner. The chimneys have been rebuilt, but are in their original locations. Photograph by the author.

more elaborate version of a familiar house plan gaining a wide following among the rising middle classes. The two-story-with-ell house, whether of central-hall or lobby-entry plan, single- or double-pile, defined modern domestic architecture in southeastern New England in this period.

Sutton builders, whether constructing one or two stories, half or full houses, had an image in mind of a proper and complete house and consistently worked toward it. When the single pile with rear lean-to proved insufficient homeowners literally raised the roof, expanding the range of rooms at the back of the house to a full two stories. By the early eighteenth century, the Georgian center-hall house had emerged as another proper form for domestic arrangements. Adaptable to single- or double-pile plans, one- or two-story height, rural New England builders added the plan, and variations on it, to their repertoires near the end of that century. From the exterior there was little to distinguish the center-hall plan from other plan-types with paired chimneys. Like present-day architectural surveyors, rural improvers may have assumed that the myriad of new two-story dwellings they beheld all contained the wasteful, conspicuous, and hitherto genteel center hall. They also could hardly have failed to observe that the builders had broken with nearly two centuries of American practice when they took to rearing full hall-and-parlor houses in one build as the general rule rather than as the exception.

Sutton homeowners at the turn of the eighteenth century favored bilaterally symmetrical plans, either center-hall or lobby-entry, with at least one ell projecting from the side or back of the house. Each plan type, distinguished from one another primarily by the use to which the central core was put, had its own variations. In the Georgian-derived plans, the central hall was immutable. Builders varied the type by constructing single- and double-pile versions. In the double-pile plan, the center hall sometimes ran only half the depth, sometimes the full two-room depth of the house.

Salmon Burdon and Timothy Burnap Jr. built center-hall houses on their farms in 1813 and 1815 respectively. Both successful farmers with land holdings surpassing the local average, their houses illustrate the possibility of variation within the limits of a recognized and familiar form (figs. 11, 12). The Burdons chose to build a two-story, single-pile main block with an integral rear ell. The center hall opened onto the two front rooms and led directly to the ell. They located their chimney stacks in the end walls of the main house and in the middle of the ell. The hipped roof and paired windows on the end wall, characteristic of full double-pile Georgian structures, belie the abbreviated form of this dwelling. The Burnaps also constructed a two-story, center-hall house with rear ell, but with a two-room-deep main block and a gable roof. Paired interior chimneys in the main house served front and back rooms. The ell had its own stack, again located about midway down its length at the back of the room closest to the big house.

In the second plan type, derived from the center-chimney tradition, the lobby-entry and hall-parlor arrangement remained constant, but the chimney location varied. Some Sutton clients chose to retain the center chimney, constructing their double-pile, hall-parlor houses in good eighteenth-century form. Others chose one of two variations—either a single-pile, hall-parlor house with paired rear chimney stacks, and in this sample an invariable integral rear ell; or a double-pile plan with end chimneys, the central core occupied by stairs and living or storage space.

The single-pile-with-rear-chimney-stacks form is well illustrated by a group of four houses built between about 1811 and 1826. Built on one of two

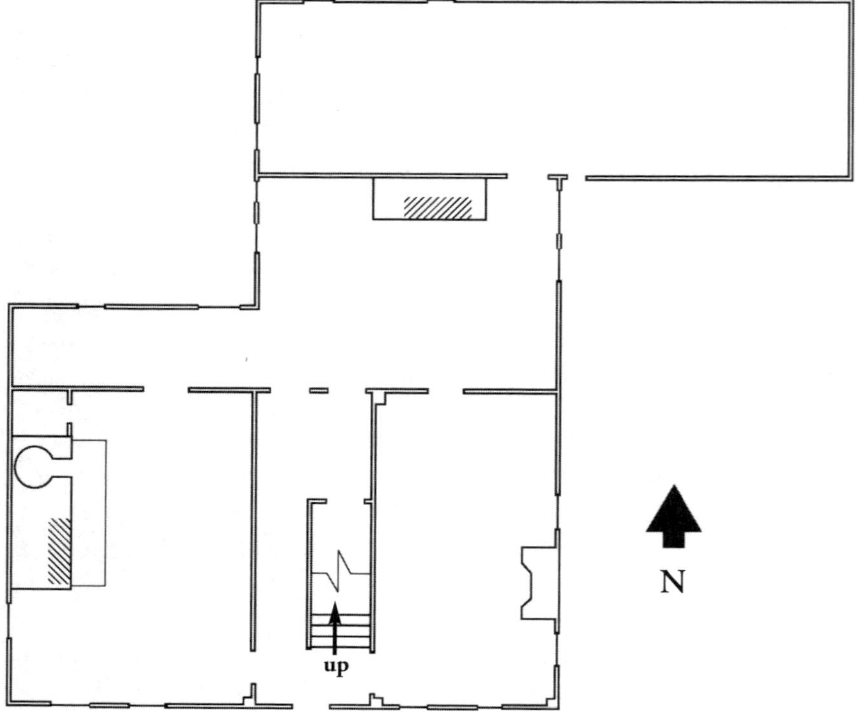

Fig. 11   Burdon house, plan. Drawing by the author.

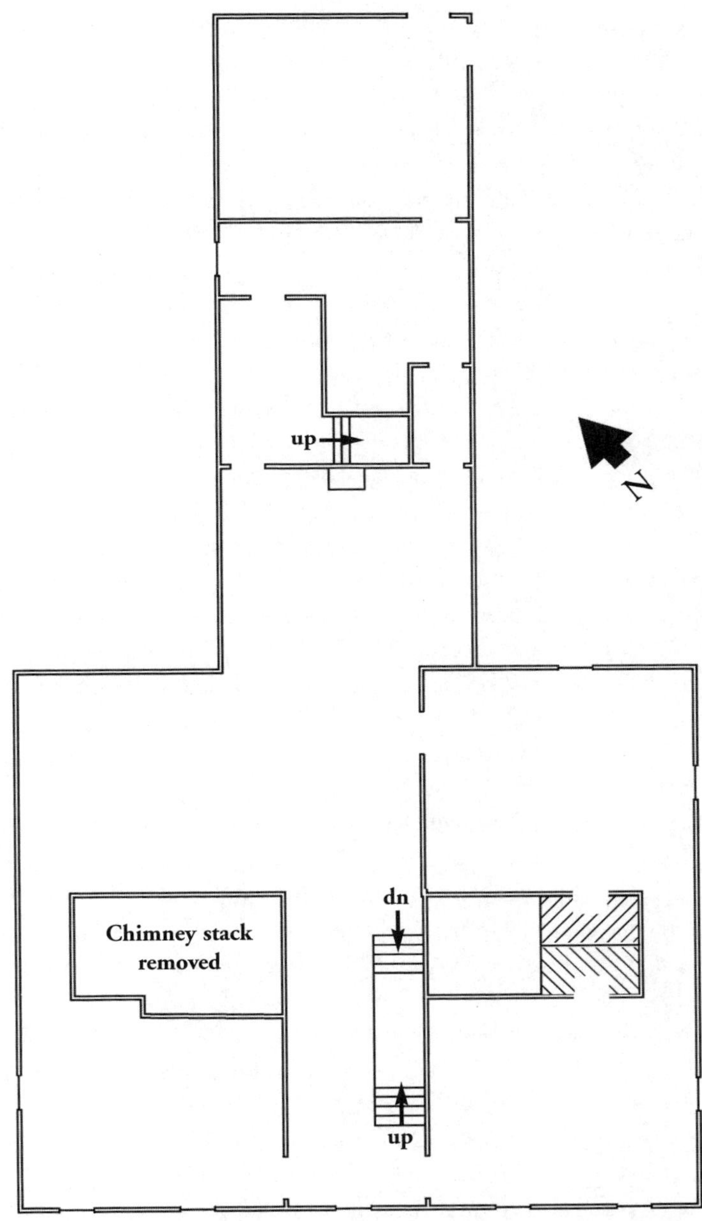

Fig. 12 Burnap house, plan. Drawing by the author.

major east-west roads in town, they served originally as homes for a trader, a teamster turned farmer, a mill agent/tanner, and an attorney. Fully Georgian in exterior appearance, these houses retained entry lobbies with dogleg stairs. A small room occupied the space behind the lobby and staircase, normally reserved for the chimney stack in such arrangements. The paired rear chimney stacks occupied the same position such stacks would occupy in a double-pile plan such as the one employed by Timothy Burnap. In each of these houses, one of the stacks served both the rear ell and the front room. Given the proclivity of eighteenth-century builders of "half-houses" to build with an eye to future expansion, the ease of expanding to a double-pile may have been a consideration in the chimney placement.

The avoidance of the very popular center-hall plan in larger double-pile form suggests conservatism on the part of client or builder. Perhaps these were the people who took the adage "waste not, want not" to heart. Joshua Armsby Jr., a housewright, and presumably the designer and contractor for his own dwelling (dated about 1820), built himself a double-pile, lobby-entry house. From his lobby rose a steep straight-run, fully enclosed stair, the width of the central core reduced to the width of the staircase. Armsby's inspiration for such an arrangement may always be a mystery, but that he was not alone in this plan solution can be seen in the description of "the farmer's cottage" in Minard Lafever's 1820 *The Young Builder's General Instructor.* Lafever presented a lobby-entry, hall-parlor arrangement with a rear service ell that incorporated the kitchen. In his descriptive text he argued that farmhouses tended to be too large, and that "a wide hall running through the house in any direction is room lost, and an opening for the reception of cold in the winter, and no material benefit arising from it in the summer season."[20] Surely these are the sentiments of a true northerner. While not unheard of, the Armsby arrangement seems to represent a deviation from more popular modernizations of the lobby plan.

A passerby might mistake Armsby's house, with its paired interior chimneys and five-bay symmetrical façade, for any of a number of more usual plan types. The exterior adhered to its own aesthetic standards and was suited to central-hall or lobby-entry plans of whatever ilk. All new houses were built with bilaterally symmetrical façades, sometimes five-bay, sometimes three-bay. Many old houses in town underwent remodeling at the turn of the eighteenth century, and all were fitted with the symmetrical fenestration. Standardized disposition of doors and windows hints at a regularizing of interior arrangements that never materialized. While rooms may have become more symmetrically arranged around a central core than they had been in the eighteenth century, the variety of plans attests to the individualized solutions to meeting modern aesthetic standards and domestic needs. Modern design principles, modified by longstanding practice, guided both interior and exterior design.

This mixture of conservatism and modernism is well illustrated in the Zadok Woodbury house, built around 1835. Woodbury, carriage-maker and gentleman, constructed a two-story, double-pile, hall-parlor, lobby-entry dwelling west of Sutton's town center, on the Boston post road. A chimney stack emerges from the center of the roofline suggesting that here is a very late survival of the traditional center-chimney form. In reality, however, two chimney stacks come together in the attic, forming a brick arch, and emerge from the roof as a single stack. The twin stacks served stoves in the front rooms on the first and second floors, a bake oven in the simply detailed east front room of the first floor, and a small fireplace in the rear range of rooms. A walk-in pantry, complete with built-in shelves, occupied the first-floor space that would have been consumed by chimney in a traditional stack arrangement.

By looking at Burdon's, Burnap's, Armsby's, and Woodbury's houses only as variations on well-established plan types, we miss the full extent of their modernity, for an integral part of all of these houses of the early national period was the ell. By 1800 the ell had become an invariable component of new rural houses, older houses were rapidly acquiring them, and they appear to have been commonplace on urban houses. Builders in the Connecticut River valley of western Massachusetts adopted the form in the last quarter of the eighteenth century. Ritchie Garrison has documented the appearance of the ell form there by 1775, and notes its rise in popularity in the last two decades of the eighteenth century. Marla Miller's work on the Porter-Phelps-Huntington house in Hadley, Massachusetts, dates the addition of an ell to the older house to 1771. The single-pile version with rear ell became a popular house form for artisans in Portsmouth, New Hampshire, by the first decade of the nineteenth century.[21] Builders constructed ells of one- or one-and-a-half-story height, to the side or to the rear of the main house. Ells solved a number of problems in the Revolution era with its economic, cultural, and social upheavals. Aesthetically, they suited the Georgian and Federal forms better than the old lean-to. A lean-to, whether to the rear or side of a building, destroyed the symmetry of roofline and profile crucial to Georgian aesthetics, which by this time permeated vernacular building. An ell permitted the main house block to speak for itself aesthetically, while also conveying the separation of public and private, or formal and service functions that characterized modern living. While the wealthy had been building Georgian mansions with wings or hyphens for seventy-five years by this point, the perceived necessity of having distinct spaces for distinct activities was of recent origin among the "industrious classes," its increasing popularity coinciding with the diversification of economic pursuits in rural families and the consequent need for functionally specific spaces. Ells, in other words, represented convenience, one of the two principles of modern building. Farmers had always arranged their houses to some standard of convenience, but in the post-Revolution house convenience became an explicit element of modern life, a moral imperative as well as a physical arrangement that bespoke personal and fiscal integrity.

While many Enlightenment thinkers and their successors believed in the absolute beauty of classical forms and detail, the definition of beauty encompassed more than the mere presence of the orders and their elements. Used improperly, or arrayed on a clumsy building even the vocabulary of the ancients could fail to create a beautiful structure. In order to be beautiful, a building or landscape must also adhere to the principles of convenience. According to this theory, convenience was not merely a means of achieving efficiency, it was a basic design element. It pertained to entire farmsteads or estates as well as individual buildings. Beauty and convenience derived not just from symmetrical arrangement and classical detail, but from the relationship of all parts of a building or complex to one another. Convenience figured prominently in English agricultural writings as early as the mid-seventeenth century when agriculturalist John Worlidge penned the opening poem to his *Systema Agriculturae*, "First cast your eye upon a Rustick Seat, / built strong and plain, yet well contriv'd and neat."[22] Its integration into architectural theory and design is unmistakable in the mid-eighteenth-century work of architectural theorist Robert Morris. A strong advocate of the chasteness of the new classicism, Morris taught the importance of convenience to neoclassical design. In his 1757 architectural treatise he insisted that the siting and arrangement of buildings be based on convenience, proportion and regularity.[23] By the late eighteenth century English architects had combined convenience and beauty to create model farms of neoclassical design. Historian John Martin Robinson called these farms syntheses of "utilitarianism and neoclassicism," and found them to be a "striking expression of [the] relationship between art and science, practical economics and philosophical ideas."[24] As rural reformers and architectural practitioners in America imbibed many of these same principles, beauty and convenience, art and science, and morality and economy became inseparable.

In the new United States all manner of publications reminded the reading public of the indispensable nature of convenience and its relationship to beauty. In his 1793 morality tale, *The Farmer's Friend,* minister Enos Hitchcock housed one of his characters, "an extensive landholder, and very respectable farmer," in "a neat and convenient edifice."[25] In 1806 Asher Benjamin noted that in architecture, "Strength, convenience and beauty are the principle things to be attended to."[26] Presumably his "elevation of a house intended for a country situation" possessed those qualities (fig. 13). Here Benjamin depicted a two-story symmetrical central block with side ells. One wing contained the entry and library while the other contained the kitchen. How this achieved the ideal of convenience, Benjamin leaves to the reader to discern, but S. W. Johnson's *Rural Economy* of the same year suggests that an aesthetic of convenience existed. In that work Johnson equated convenience with stability and a low-lying profile, and beauty with the appearance of convenience.[27] Benjamin's country house embodied stability in its two-story central block, an anchor of sorts between the less substantial ells, and incorporated a low-lying profile in its wings, which any passerby would have recognized as containing workspaces, or spaces not central to the public, social functions of the house. Containing those two elements, it must, by Johnson's definition, have been convenient; appearing convenient, it must have been beautiful.

Fig. 13 "Elevation for a house which is intended for a country situation." From Asher Benjamin, *The American Builder's Companion,* plate 54. 6th edition. Boston: R. P. and C. Williams, 1827. Reprint, Dover Publications, 1969. Reprinted with permission of Dover Publications, Inc.

Professional architects and reformers alike sounded the clarion call of convenience well into the century. Mrs. L. C. Tuthill only gave voice to an already popular sentiment when she wrote in 1848, "The leading principle in Architecture is fitness for the end designed. Utility, convenience, and propriety are included in the term fitness."[28] Architect Robert Mills (1781–1855), taking up the theme in his undated autobiographical notes, wrote that his designs were based on the principle that "beauty is founded upon order, and . . . convenience and utility were constituent parts. In the cases of private buildings it is of special importance that convenience, utility and economy should be associated."[29] The combination of physical attributes of convenience with the modern interpretation of classical elements created house forms that gave this era of domestic building its distinctive character. Convenience, like the chaste neoclassical forms, implied order and economy of effort as well as of money.

The beauty and convenience of the classical ell house are well illustrated by the Phelps-Stockwell house, dated about 1806, one of the earliest extant Sutton farmhouses to exhibit all of the most popular external attributes of a modern dwelling—two stories, bilaterally symmetrical façade, paired end chimneys, and ell. Enoch Stockwell purchased the sixty-five–acre farm in the Eight Lots District of Sutton in1806. On the home lot stood a new house, stylish and spacious, the epitome of all that characterized modern rural dwellings (fig. 14). Two stories tall and one room deep, the exterior of the main house presented a tall, slim, Federal profile to passersby. End chimneys punctuated the gables. A one-story, center-chimney, gambrel-roofed house built around 1767 served as side ell. The new house was not as far removed from the old ell as first appearances might suggest. Beneath that façade of modernity lay not only the customary hall-parlor plan, with entry lobby and dogleg stair, but a heavy timber frame that the builder of the gambrel-roofed house would have recognized.

Because the old house has been gutted, we cannot say exactly how the Stockwells used their ell, but we do know that by 1836 two families occupied the dwelling. Palmer Harback had married Stockwell's daughter, Abigail Russell, in 1832, and the couple came to live at the Stockwell farm before 1836. On Enoch's death, Harback was to have half the produce of the farm, the running of which he was to oversee. The layering of modern and traditional practice in the Stockwell house offers us a glimpse of the extent to which these people remained grounded in their past while adapting to new social and economic conditions. The big house differed only superficially in plan from its pre-Revolution counterparts, but its massing changed dramatically as southern

Fig. 14 Phelps/Stockwell house, front façade. The original single-story, gambrel-roofed eighteenth-century house was remodeled as a side ell. Photograph by the author.

New Englanders adopted the single-pile, two-story big house with side or rear ells. In like manner, the framing changed only slowly, but increasing numbers of farmers and artisans reared whole houses complete with appendages in a single build, rather than gradually achieving a recognized "full" house through decades of accretions. This symmetrical house with fenestration and chimney stacks placed to achieve balance rather than to accommodate interior arrangements, seemingly so orderly and refined, contained a welter of activities that pressed most rooms into service, negating the Georgian ideal of separation of work and leisure, or of public and private, and rendering the improvers' worries over wasted space pointless.

Rural reformers, unlike architects, tended to divorce the beauty of convenience from any architectural ornament or style. Instead they emphasized the beauty that arose naturally from "well contriv'd" situations and from simplicity. They made women's role in creating and maintaining these convenient spaces explicit, as well as her guilt when her household failed to achieve this ideal, thus offering us an opportunity to examine women's roles in the transformation of their dwellings and home lots into beautiful and convenient spaces. In the reformers' view, farmers held the key to public and national virtue in the early republic, but their spouses held the key to private or domestic virtue. Just as farmers needed to practice economy and restraint in the management of their farms and most particularly in the construction of their houses, farm wives were expected to exercise the same qualities in their household and family affairs. In the atmosphere of increasingly personal and sentimentalized republicanism that emerged in the late eighteenth century, in which frugality, simple tastes, and manners became identified with feminine virtues, what better way to ensure public virtue than through private felicity?[30] Hitchcock's main protagonist in *The Farmer's Friend,* Mr. Charles Worthy, would never have been able to maintain his comfortable frontier home without the inestimable Mrs. Worthy. Matching her husband in frugality and industriousness, she oversaw the maintenance of plain, neat, and clean rooms, utensils, and furniture. She made all her own window curtains and seat cushions, and it was undoubtedly she who planted the dooryard with honeysuckle, sweetbriar, a rose tree, and a jessamine. With this description, Hitchcock, like Johnson, alludes to the aesthetic of convenience. Unlike Johnson, however, this aesthetic was based on simplicity and the fruits of nature. Simplicity and her garden united, in this story, to create beauty and convenience and to make Mrs. Worthy's life on the frontier one of relative ease.

Nearly three decades later domestic economist Hannah Barnard also defined convenience and heralded its benefits in her 1820 *Dialogues on Domestic and Rural Economy.* As the overextended Prinks family strove to save themselves from bankruptcy, father Prinks built a shed from the kitchen to the cow shed "to make it more convenient for Ma to milk in wet weather."[31] Barnard contrasted the nearly destitute family, brought to that point by Mrs. Prinks's own extravagance, with Mrs. Prinks's brother's family. The brother presided over a well-paved and always clean cow yard, while his wife oversaw the immaculate and spare house, devoid of dirt-collecting carpets, all her utensils properly cleaned, oiled, and stored. Convenient, simple building forms and household utensils translated into economy of effort that, for Mrs. Barnard, led naturally to fiscal responsibility and created a beauty of its own, quite distinct from any beauty that may have derived from architectural ornament.

Convenience did not necessarily translate into the aesthetic of spareness, as promoted by Hitchcock and Barnard, in the New England countryside, but it did assume a particular form, and women appear to have been the primary beneficiaries of this new desire for convenience which translated into a two-story house with ell. Many of the new houses, in spite of their two stories, had no more rooms in the main body of the dwelling than had the traditional double-pile, one-story structures. Built with only two rooms down and two rooms up, these blocks tended to occupy less than 900 square feet in plan. Their ells, however, put them close to or over the 1,000 square feet that represented the high end of the normal scale at the end of the eighteenth century.

The Jonathan Dudley Jr. house, built in the 1810s, was typical of the type. Built on the same plan as at least three other extant houses constructed between 1811 and 1825 in Sutton, the main block of the two-story, single-pile dwelling occupied 702 square feet. The integral rear ell added an additional 248 square feet (fig. 15). The independent roofing system, separate entrance, and generally lower height relative to the main block, gave the ell the appearance of being a distinct little house. Larger ells with their own chimney stacks appeared to function as independent service wings, thus implying the fulfillment of the Georgian ideal of the main house serving the formal and social needs of the family while relegating services and servants to subsidiary wings or detached buildings. The appearance of such an arrangement may be only in the mind of the modern scholar, however, for contemporary observers surely never would have made a distinction between home life and work in the rural New England household. Both house and wing, as well as subsidiary exterior spaces, were devoted to activities that sustained the rural family.

Several Sutton examples illustrate the evolution of the ell house into a model of modern convenience, an important tool in economizing women's labor at a time when household help was difficult to get and keep. An early attempt at making the house a more convenient workspace may be seen in Malachi Marble's addition of a small rear lean-to to his mid- to late-eighteenth-century house sometime before his death in 1810. This single-room lean-to, called a "well room" by the administrators of his estate, appended formerly detached necessities to the house, without substantially altering the dwelling's functions or circulation patterns. The lean-to incorporated a three-seat privy and woodshed in the cellar, and a water pump on the first floor. At the time of his death, Malachi's widow still set her cheeses in an upstairs room of the house, designated the cheese chamber, and set her milk in the buttery on the first floor in a room adjacent to the well room. In short, the lean-to addition removed none of the service functions from the house, but by bringing water and wood within doors, eased Mrs. Marble's labors considerably.

The ell that Moses Putnam built in 1806 at the request of his father Nathaniel also served to extend the functions of their shared house, rather

Fig. 15a   Jonathan Dudley Jr. house, front façade. Photograph by the author.

Fig. 15b   Jonathan Dudley Jr. house, plan. Drawing by the author.

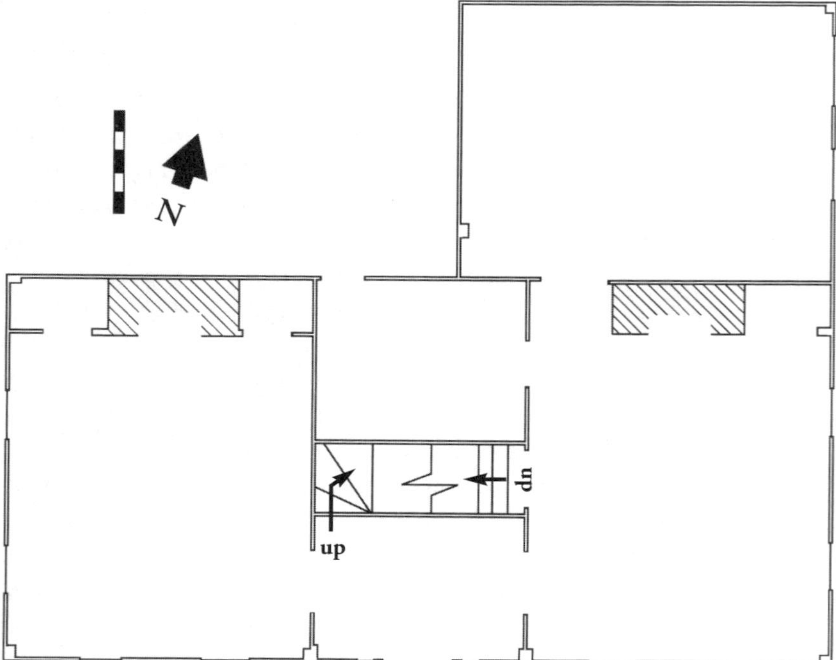

Fig. 16 | Putnam house, with 1806 side ell. Photograph by the author.

than remove services from the main body of the house (fig. 16). The Putnam's ell consisted of a "small house, wood house, milk room."[32] What Nathaniel meant by "small house" remains a mystery, but clearly storage of wood and processing of milk required distinct spaces that could not be accommodated in the old house.[33] The big house retained its two large kitchens, one in the front of the house and one in the rear of the house, both with bake ovens and large hearths. In 1807, Moses partially enclosed the rear hearth to accommodate a set kettle, the purchase of which he recorded in his farm accounts. The set kettle became an important piece of technology in the increasingly efficient rural household, being used by both farmer and farmwife. In such a piece of equipment women could boil water for laundry or prepare dye-stuffs, and farmers could prepare large quantities of boiled feed for livestock.

Zadok Woodbury's 1835–38 complex illustrates the ell as efficient, but not self-sufficient, workspace. The entire lot as reconstructed by Woodbury illuminates the interwoven patterns of home and work life, through the placement of structures on the house lot as well as through the use of rooms within the house (fig. 17). When Zadok bought the Jonathan Woodbury farm in 1835, an old house and barn stood on the property somewhere on the opposite side of the Boston post road from his new house lot. By 1841 Zadok had removed the old buildings from the homestead and constructed farm structures adjacent to his new house. The Woodburys' house lot contained a shed or shop at the northwest corner of the house and a New England barn with an attached carriage shed just west of the shop. Attached to the east end of the main house, and set back from the front façade, was a story-and-a-half, double-pile ell. The detached shop at the northwest corner of the house and the extension of the ell to the north of the rear house façade formed an enclosed rear yard, convenient to both men's and women's realms of production. The Woodburys' arrangement of house and house lot indicate a very modern concern for efficiency or convenience.

The front room of the ell seems to have been the hub of all housework. The plentiful natural light from the four windows on the east and south walls suited this spacious room to any number of daily women's tasks, from sewing to food preparation. At the east end of the room stood the chimney stack, with its small fireplace, bake oven, and set kettle. Not two feet from the set kettle

Fig. 17　　Zadok Woodbury house and lot, c. 1835. House and barn are oriented to the road and face south. Woodbury built this complex with all the modern conveniences, including a New England barn and side ell on his house. From Benedict and Tracy, *History of the Town of Sutton.*

was a well. From this room Mrs. Woodbury and her adopted daughter had easy access to a number of other work areas. Across the room to the west were the stairs to the cellar, in which was located the dairy room. The Woodburys partitioned this space off from the rest of the cellar with plastered brick walls, and finished the floor with flagstones. Shelves built into the brick piers of the main chimney stack provided storage space. The rear room of the ell served as the woodshed, its interior remaining unfinished until the late 1980s. This very efficient space also adjoined the east room of the main house, with its bake oven and large, walk-in pantry.

The interdependence of ell and big house, house and yards, is evident in the paths of women's chores. The Woodbury women divided their housework among the southeast hall of the big house, the cellar beneath the big house and the ell. If they were like most New England farmwomen, their duties included caring for fowl, milking cows, and tending substantial garden plots. They therefore regularly used barns, outbuildings, and yards. The close proximity of house and outbuildings on the Woodbury house lot reflects this integrated pattern of work. The specialized workspace in the ell, and the amount of house room devoted to women's work indicates the continued importance of women's work in the overall household economy even as industrialization was removing many traditional women's jobs from the house.

The closest approximation to the Georgian ideal in Sutton was probably the Lazarus LeBaron house. If anyone commanded enough capital and labor to separate their social and work lives, the LeBarons did. Even in their magnificent home lot, however, we see the economic interrelationship of big house, ell, outbuildings, and yards, and hence, the extent of women's involvement in the household economy and the integrated nature of that economy.

LeBaron died in November 1827 leaving his fourth wife a very large estate. As was customary, appraisers came in to inventory the estate and to determine the widow's portion or dower. Mary Woodbury LeBaron received the garden and close yard with two small barns, a piece of pastureland adjacent to the homestead, and two outlying properties. In addition she retained the portion of the house in which she then lived, that being the southwest and northeast rooms (or front left parlor and right rear room) on the first floor, the chambers above those rooms, and the garrets over those, and sufficient room in the cellar for her uses. The appraisers also gave her a "privilege in the back part of the house to do all necessary work with a part of the cheese room or Buttery," a right to the well, and privileges through all house passageways, the door yard, around the barn, and to the "Back house." Because none of the rooms allotted to her contained a bake oven, the reference in the probate document to the back part of the house with cheese room or buttery, may refer to the northeast room of the main house, where the fireplace did contain a bake oven. While some of the dower acknowledged the Widow LeBaron's right to income from productive property, much of it recognized her own role in the productivity of the household. The duties of the female head of the household took her beyond the parlor into all areas of the house where unprocessed or processed foodstuffs and household goods might be stored and worked. Mrs. LeBaron was no lady of leisure. Her responsibilities took her to the cellar and garret, and out to the barns and gardens. The success of the LeBaron enterprises depended to a great extent on her ability, at the very least, to process or oversee the processing of, the products of field, barn, and garden for household use, and perhaps for market.

There is no question that the LeBarons' ell housed service functions. There is also no question that much of the rest of the house, even in this privileged household, continued to serve as work areas. Re-visualized as a tool employed to further household economic strategies, the rural dwelling assumes a complex financial and laboring dimension that Andrew Jackson Downing and his predecessors, the rural reformers, denied or ignored in their promotion of the simple, domestic, and rustic life of the countryside.

In building two-story houses with attached wings, the artisans, farmers, and emerging professionals of central Massachusetts did not ape urban mannerisms or imitate the traditional gentry. Instead, they drew material symbols of their station in society and life from the only grammar available to them. Over the course of the eighteenth century two-story, bilaterally symmetrical dwellings had come to symbolize success and stature. They also connoted a segregation and ordering of activities not found in older domestic arrangements, but deemed increasingly desirable, if not obtainable, by an ever-broader spectrum of society in the early republic.

Far from leading the retired, bucolic life that rural reformers seemed to envision for country folk, the builders of these houses lived in a working landscape, their dwellings enmeshed in yards, fields, and manufacturing sites that all figured in the economic strategies of farmers. The reordering of the farmscape extended well beyond the house, encompassing door yards, barns and barn yards, miscellaneous outbuildings and fields, and shops and mills. If the houses conveyed New England farmers' status as citizens of a new republic, as respectable participants in a national community, then their barns and fields, shops and mills surely testified to their status as successful participants in the local and regional economy.

Chapter 4

The Industrious Rural Landscape

Sutton celebrated the nation's centennial with the publication of one of the best local histories of the period. A rich accumulation of local facts and records, it also offers superb insight into the late-nineteenth-century perspective on the olden days. When the Reverends Mr. Benedict and Mr. Tracy looked back over the 172-year history of their community, they found much to celebrate, but also more than a little to bemoan.

> The trade in th[e] old store was very different from the trade of the present time, and the traders there all became rich. They took in farmers' produce, and sent a team to Boston every week. . . . They bought beef, pork, butter, cheese, grain, poultry, eggs, wool, feathers, flax and in fine any thing that the farmers then raised. Farming was a business. The *farmers of New England then* supplied the Boston market, and Sutton did her part. The railroads had not then injured farming interests in the eastern states. . . . The old church stood nearly opposite this store. It had no fireplace—it was before the day of stoves—yet the people attended church more then than now. The women used to carry foot-stoves, filled with coals in the forenoon from their own fire-places; then at noon-time they would replenish them from the friendly hearths around the church, and no one suffered from cold.[1]

The world that Benedict and Tracy looked back on so nostalgically had taken shape in their grandparents' generation, but by 1876 the years of the early republic had come to stand for venerable, immutable tradition. Before the railroads all the farmers and merchants had been rich; before the stove, all the people had been happy and god-fearing, or at least reverent. But if we look back before the railroad's arrival in 1847 to a time when the stove had only just begun to intrude upon the hearth, we find that in spite of the lack of the most obvious icons of the industrial age, every aspect of Sutton life was being transformed by industrialization. That process took the form of exploitation of abundant waterways for the power required to run manufacturing operations, and of the exploitation of human labor to supply goods that the manufacturers needed, from agricultural products to handcrafted machine parts. Furthermore, the farm life of yore evoked by the good ministers was a condition of that industrializing economy, not an exception to it. Benedict and Tracy were quite right when they observed nostalgically that back then farming was a business. But they apparently meant that one could earn a good living solely by exchanging locally the raw, or minimally processed, produce of the farm. While they acknowledged the Boston market, forty-odd miles to the east, they made no suggestion that Sutton farmers produced for any broader market, or that farmers and artisans alike produced non-agricultural goods for sale far beyond the borders of Sutton. Their ancestors transformed the landscape, however, to accommodate a very different business of farming than Benedict and Tracy envisioned. That landscape accommodated agricultural and manufacturing pursuits cheek by jowl. The physical proximity and overlap of these enterprises matched their economic interdependence, an interdependence derived not only from farmers producing foodstuffs for the growing number of non-farmers, but also from farm families manufacturing a variety of goods for local markets and beyond.

Tracy and Benedict were only part of a larger trend toward romanticization of the New England landscape in the late nineteenth and early twentieth centuries. Our understanding of that landscape is skewed not only because much of the contemporary prescriptive and popular literature chose to ignore the commercial aspects of rural life, but also because, much later, commentators and observers devised their own myth of country life in early New England and set about preserving those parts of the landscape that reinforced that myth.[2] The result was an image in the public mind of a sometimes wild, but always picturesque Olde New England, devoid of commercialism, pre-dating the scars of late-nineteenth-century industrialization. It was, of course, a lie. Much of the landscape on which that bucolic myth was based developed precisely at the time that rural New Englanders were immersing themselves in an increasingly commercial and industrial economy.[3] This economic transformation manifested itself not only in rebuilt and reorganized domestic spaces, but also in a farmscape rebuilt along the same principles as the houses. Driven by economic opportunity or necessity, New England farm families had to decide how best to reorganize their working landscape to accommodate new work patterns as well as new cultural expectations for order and visual manifestations of efficiency. In reality, it did not require only convenience and economy to succeed in the New England countryside. Whether farmer or artisan, rural or urban resident, success in the northeast required an understanding of the exigencies of the new industrializing economy. The conflicts and accommodations generated in rural areas by the transition to that industrial economy have been documented in Gary Kulik's work on riparian rights in Rhode Island and Jonathan Prude's investigation of the contentious relationships between mills and town government in southeastern Massachusetts. Thomas Dublin was instrumental in linking the rural New England economy to the urban economy through his analysis of the outwork systems devised by urban merchants and manufacturers, and Prude presented the countryside not just as adjunct to urban economic developments, but as the nexus, since it was there that water-powered industries grew.[4] In the midst of all this, farmers frequently found themselves denigrated as backward, non-improvers who refused to take advantage of new and wondrous farming tools and techniques. As in the eighteenth century, however, the touted reforms worked better in other places, under different economic and labor systems, and often were not well suited to New England's farm economy. The fact is that New England farmers did innovate in their own way, imposing order on their yards and their fields and adopting a new work tool that promised to benefit them more than all the new hay rakes and plows coming out of their own shops—the New England barn. The timing of the general acceptance of the new barn form, as well as of house ells, coincided not only with the ascendancy of notions of economy and convenience, but also with the increased industrialization of the Blackstone River valley and the changes in the agricultural market that accompanied that industrialization.

The visual character and productiveness of farmland came under close scrutiny in the fervor of post-Revolution improvement. Just as a slovenly house could not contain anything but slovenly residents, a sloppy farm could not possibly be a productive one. Early in the nineteenth century, the perceived slovenliness of eighteenth-century fields gave way to a landscape carefully bounded by permanent stone walls or neat wooden fences. Although some of the patterns of pre-Revolution farm fields have survived in rural New England, the character of those fields has not. For descriptions of agricultural conditions prior to the great post-Revolution rebuilding we must turn to the recorded observations of contemporaries. In his mid-eighteenth-century work on New

England husbandry, Jared Eliot not only extolled the virtues of farming, but also assessed the condition of the region's countryside.[5] Eliot acknowledged that New Englanders had made progress in the arts of farming and manufacturing, cattle and horse breeding, but maintained that that progress had come in spite of 130 years of wasteful methods of cultivation and clearing. For the most part, New Englanders overworked and under-manured their fields, and failed to recognize the potential productivity of lands categorized as wastelands—marshes, swamps, and bogs.

William Logan, a wealthy Quaker merchant of Philadelphia and one of Eliot's correspondents, echoed his assessment of the state of New England agriculture. After a trip to the region in 1755, Logan sent his impressions of New England husbandry to Eliot, "I Cant say I met with anything Instructive relating to Farming in your Parts. I think the Contrary, and that Slovenlyness [*sic*] too generally prevails and that Nature does more for your people in general than they do by any Industry." Some of Logan's assessment may be attributed to regional chauvinism, some of it to the general disdain that all gentlemen seemed to hold for working farmers, but his observation of meadows that needed watering and swamps that needed draining were telling, in light of what would come later.[6]

The author of *American Husbandry,* who signed his work only as "An American," reiterated Eliot's and Logan's bleak assessments of New England agriculture. Written after 1766 and published in 1775, the work intended to highlight the products of the colonies and the importance of those goods to the economy of the motherland.[7] After a summary of the marketable goods of the region, the anonymous "American" began his geographic description of New England in the euphoric tones of a writer of pastoral: "The face of the country has in general a cultivated, inclosed, and cheerful prospect; the farmhouses are well and substantially built, and stand thick; gentlemen's houses appear every where, and have an air of a wealthy and contented people."[8] The author's own recommendations for furthering husbandry in New England reveal the extent of his poetic license in introducing the reader to the region. With the backhanded compliment that "cultivated parts of New England are more regularly inclosed than Canada," he begins to provide the reader with his true perception of the unfulfilled promise of the region's agriculture.[9]

Although more regularly bounded than the farms of their northern neighbors, the New England "planters do not sufficiently attend to this circumstance; many estates and farms are in this respect in such condition that in Great Britain they would be thought in a state of devastation." Furthermore, on many more farms only the house and its yards were enclosed, "the rest lie like common fields in England." When they did enclose, he complained, New England farmers preferred posts and rails or boards to the live hedges used by progressive English agriculturalists. Not only were the fields' boundaries in a derelict state, but the fields themselves were deplorable, the result of the worst plowing "An American" had ever seen.[10] The list of deficiencies went on to include the tools, which were terrible, and the livestock, which were badly treated. New Englanders had not acquired the system of crop rotation, livestock penning, and field manuring advocated by Eliot and the English agricultural writers, for the "American" commented that they would never acquire enough manure for raising turnips and other root crops for feed while they allowed their cattle to range through the woods.

Value judgments aside, these authors describe a landscape of unbounded fields, wandering livestock, and non-intensive land use. Population and market pressures had not yet reached a point where New Englanders felt compelled to transform wasteland into productive land, and to harness even animal waste in the drive to make fields and livestock pay a handsome profit. That began to change with the threats to capital and investments posed by the war, as well as with the potential profits to be made as a result of that same conflict.

The Marquis de Chastellux traveled through New England in the early 1780s and noted a trend to agricultural improvement. This he attributed to the loss of commerce occasioned by the war, with the consequence being that wealthy men from the coastal cities put their capital into agricultural land in the interior. Indeed, land records bear out the Marquis's assessment. The Hancocks—Thomas and John—owned over sixty acres of land and a house in Sutton, among other locations in Worcester County, throughout the revolutionary period. In Sutton, they held property from 1763 to 1785. The income from these and other farms may have helped see the Hancocks through the wartime devastations wreaked on Boston and its environs. When the Marquis passed through Grafton, adjacent to Sutton, he found a great number of meadows "intersected and watered by trenches cut on purpose." Mr. Gale, tavernkeeper and owner of some of the meadows, told the Marquis that some of them yielded four tons of hay an acre, with the after-grass going to dairy cattle. Chastellux also commented on the road between West Hartford and Farmington, Connecticut, which he found graced with houses dispersed and grouped, adorned with trees and meadows, in such a manner that it had the appearance of "a garden, in the English style, [such] as it would be difficult for art to imitate."[11]

According to the English agricultural improvers, acknowledged internationally as leaders in scientific methods of farming, an enclosed countryside translated into a profitable countryside. Jared Eliot praised the benefits of enclosure well before the Revolution, reprinting a laudatory account of the well-established Norfolk, England, system of enclosure in his fourth essay. Ultimately, that essay makes clear how unsuited dreams of an English system of cultivation were to the New England colonies, and helps to explain why New England fields looked slovenly to eighteenth-century observers. The author concluded that with the new method of agriculture, "There is three Times as much Work for the Labourers, in Ploughing, Sowing, Threshing, etc. This supports almost twice as many Families, who have almost twice as much Work. . . ."[12] Hired labor, or people who would classify themselves as laborers, was a precious commodity in eighteenth-century New England. The country's inhabitants had no need for systems that created three times the work, but did nothing to increase land ownership. Throughout most of that century, there existed no necessity or incentive for practicing agriculture as intensively as the English. Not until wartime profits and a fresh influx of capital from the cities made agricultural improvements attractive do we begin to see a rise in carefully bounded fields.

Shortly after the Marquis's sojourn through New England, Luigi Castiglione traveled from Boston to Lancaster in Worcester County. He observed cultivated clearings in the woods "enclosed with wooden fences or with a wall about four feet high made of boulders." Traveling from New York City to Norwalk, Connecticut, in August 1786, he observed Connecticut fields bound with stone walls. Ten years later Timothy Dwight heaped praise on the stone walls of Worcester County which he described as more extensive and better built than elsewhere in the region. Perhaps in response to criticisms about not enclosing with live hedges, and certainly mindful of the association of neat boundaries with productivity, Dwight wrote, "A farm well surrounded and divided by good stone walls presents to my mind, irresistibly, the image of tidy, skillful, profitable agriculture, and promises to me within doors the still more agreeable prospect of plenty and prosperity."[13]

The adoption of bounded fields did not happen all at once, in spite of the promise of greater productivity and profits. Stone walls initially marked house lots, and farmers continued to employ post-and-rail or board fences well into the nineteenth century.[14] By the end of the eighteenth century, however, stone walls increasingly defined fields and property boundaries. The language of land deeds marks the gradual explicit delineation of field, yard, and property.

For much of the 1700s abutters, roads and such landmarks as heaps of stones, marked trees, ponds, and large rocks defined a property's limits. The description of land transferred from Timothy Manning, a Sutton carpenter, to Samuel Lilley, a weaver from Woodstock, Connecticut, was typical. Manning sold forty-eight acres to Lilley, bounded easterly on land of John Bates, northerly on Crooked Pond, west on land of Benjamin Marsh, and south on the county road.[15] Such a description implies a very personal acquaintance with the land and with neighbors' property. Land records that seldom mention fences and walls, much less use them as boundary markers, imply the lack of physical delineation of property lines that so dismayed eighteenth-century agricultural improvers.

The occasional references to fences in pre-revolutionary property deeds suggest their limited use. A 1732 transaction between two Sutton men described property that included "a dwelling house standing on the same, with the fence." The fence merited inclusion as a structure rather than a boundary marker. Mentioned in the same phrase as the dwelling, it probably protected the dooryard or house lot from incursions of free-ranging livestock, but did not serve to separate one landowner's property from another's. Thirty years later, deeds did occasionally use fences as markers, but acknowledged their ephemeral quality with the standard phrase "as the fence now stands."[16]

Land records cite walls more frequently near the end of the eighteenth century, but they continue to appear in association with the home lot or with the qualifier "as the wall now stands." Deeds and widows' partitions mentioned garden walls, barnyard walls, and orchard walls by the turn of the century, suggesting a trend to careful ordering of the acre or two around the house, or home lot. Not until the late 1810s and 1820s did boundary descriptions frequently incorporate walls. Such phrases as "ranging with the wall," "to a bend in the wall," "to the center of the wall," indicate clearly that stone walls had become a standard means of bounding land, and had assumed a more or less permanent place on the landscape.[17] Turn-of-the-century paintings record the order imposed on the post-Revolution landscape by this careful demarcation of boundaries. In this countryside stone walls and neat post-and-rail fences separate fields from each other, from house lots and from roads (fig. 18).[18]

Bounding land with solid walls did not require removal of earlier substantial structures, nor did it disrupt established field patterns. Without too much alteration to the old order, a new order could be superimposed. That farmers perceived a need for a new order suggests that the nature of farming had changed, a change brought about in part by population pressures on the land.

Fig. 18 | View of farm fields separated by stone walls, West Sutton. Photograph by the author.

By 1790 all of Sutton's farmland was in private hands. Its growing population had to be accommodated on a landscape that had no more public lands to divide among its inhabitants. Sutton residents reached that accommodation, at least in part, by reducing the size of their landholdings. In 1798 the average size of a taxed property was 86.77 acres. In 1830 it was 58.41 acres. Ten years later landowners held approximately eight fewer acres on average. Shrinking landholdings between 1790 and 1840 undoubtedly convinced more farmers to heed the agricultural improvers' calls for more intensive, more economic, farming methods. The shift in farm strategies is evident in the uses to which Sutton farmers put their lands.

Sutton began the nineteenth century with 41 percent of its total area devoted to farmland—that is tillage, English or upland hay, fresh meadow hay, and pasturage. By 1840 farmland consumed half of its total acreage. In those years the amount of improved land devoted to tillage ranged from 10 to almost 14 percent, pasturage consumed from 50 to 55 percent of the land, and hay from 34 to 36 percent. Within these relatively stable numbers, paradoxically, lies evidence of changing farm strategies.

In 1801 Sutton farmers grew wheat, rye, oats, corn, barley, peas and beans, and hops. Wheat and barley were already marginal products by that time, and wheat remained so for the next four decades, accounting for only 2 to 4 percent of the town's produce. By 1830 farmers had dropped peas, beans, and hops from production. In the next decade barley rose from 2 percent of the town's grain production to nearly 8 percent, with a corresponding drop in rye. Throughout this time period corn and oats remained the staple crops, accounting for between 79 and 98 percent of the grains grown. Again, however, we see a shift in strategy as corn production fell off markedly while oat production increased. Overall, Sutton farmers boosted their grain production by less than three bushels per acre in the first four decades on the nineteenth century.

A similar exchange of one product for another occurred in the hay fields. At the opening of the century English and fresh meadow hay fields were somewhat evenly distributed. English hay occupied almost 16 percent of all improved acres while fresh meadow hay occupied just over 18 percent. Over the course of the next four decades total hay field acreage increased by only 2 percent, but the amount of improved land devoted to English hay fields, a more nutritional hay than the fresh meadow hay, increased by 12 percent as fresh meadow field acreage fell off.

With only moderate increases in bushels of grain or tons of hay per acre, agricultural production in Sutton prior to 1840 had clearly not been dramatically "improved," in the sense of increased yields on the same amount of land. By the same token, strategies changed as farmers adjusted their production of venerable staple crops, and added new products such as milk, cheese, butter, and wool, in direct response to increased manufacturing in their town and throughout the Blackstone River valley. As farming strategy changed, so did the support structures necessary to sustain the new agriculture. New Englanders began to use a new barn form, noted at the time for its convenience.[19] The barns that those farmers took to building in the early years of the republic, since labeled New England barns, testify to the transformation of the farm economy. Henry David Thoreau, ever the observant commentator, concluded in the 1840s that in spite of substantial houses, his contemporaries measured a farmer's prosperity by "the degree to which the barn overshadows the house."[20]

The appearance and increased popularity of the New England barn required that a new generation both establish itself financially and come to the point of needing not only a new barn, but a new barn form. Unlike with housing, farmers jettisoned traditional barn plans completely when they modernized their farm buildings. The lack of almost any extant pre-revolutionary farm buildings may be attributed in part to their inability to serve any function in the new agricultural economy. Unfortunately, that poor survival rate also makes it more difficult to assess the extent of the transformation of the working farm environment. The eighteenth-century travelers who commented so frequently on farm fields generally ignored barns and outbuildings. Nevertheless, a profile of customary barn form and barn use emerges from modern field studies and early-nineteenth-century agricultural literature.

English barns were ubiquitous in colonial America. Traditional throughout western Europe and England, the form appeared with regional variations from the Chesapeake Bay area to Maine.[21] Generally composed of three bays, the so-called English barn contained a center drive or threshing floor, also called simply the floor. Large doors opened onto the floor at the front of the barn. The roofline ran perpendicular to the drive.

Early in the seventeenth century Massachusetts Bay colonists took to using a single English barn to accommodate both livestock and grains. One side bay stabled livestock, sometimes with a hayloft above, while the other side contained the haymow. This usage was not common in contemporary England where cow houses and hay barns were generally separate structures, nor was it universal in early New England. Some communities maintained the tradition of housing livestock separately from grains in English barns. In other settlements, people combined human habitation and grain storage in longhouse, or house-and-byre structures.[22] In still other cases, a dwelling's garret served as granary, as attested to by a 1638 building contract for a Massachusetts Bay house that read "the side bearers for the second story, being to be loaden with corn &c, must not be pinned on, but rather eyther lett in to the studs or borne up with false studds."[23] Yet even where the combined-use, three-bay English barn flourished, farmsteads contained additional structures that accommodated extra storage for grains and housing for animals such as sheep, pigs, and horses.[24]

Documentary evidence from several Connecticut River valley towns testifies to the diversity of farm outbuildings and barns in the eighteenth century. Barn sizes ranged from twenty by eighteen feet to fifty-four by seventy feet. Some buildings were long and narrow, the expected proportions for cow houses. Others, only two bays wide, evidently served a single, rather than multiple, function. The most common form, however, was the approximately 1,200 square foot, three-bay English barn.[25]

Before the end of the eighteenth century the combined-use English barn had become the most prevalent barn form in New England. Samuel Deane, an agriculturalist and minister, defined a barn in the 1790s as "a sort of house used for storing unthreshed grain, hay and straw, and all kinds of fodder." He noted that in this country farmers used those same barns to "lodge and feed beasts in, to thresh grain, dress flax, etc."[26] In the mid-1790s Timothy Dwight observed of Worcester County, in his customary boosterish tones, that "In no part of this country are the barns universally so large and so grand."[27] The presence of large barns prior to the appearance of New England barns suggests that at least some, and if we believe Dwight, even most, Worcester County residents housed their livestock and produce together. At the end of the eighteenth century New England farmsteads contained cellarless, English barns, often more than one to a site, and numerous support structures. This remained the common practice into the nineteenth century, as agricultural publications, documentary evidence, and extant structures demonstrate.[28]

An 1824 article in the *New England Farmer* offers clues to customary barn-building practice and advice on how to improve it without significantly altering the form. It described a barn of "ordinary size," built in the "usual shape," but distinguished from the run-of-the-mill barn by its neatness and tightness. This three-bay structure had two eight-foot cellars beneath the end bays for storing hay, and a cellar beneath the drive for potatoes and green fodder. The large doors opened to the south and had twelve panes of glass over them. Attached to the main building on the north or back side were the stables, "about twenty-five feet in width, thirty feet long, and twelve or fourteen feet high." Cattle entered the space from the east side, while people could enter from the barn. A cellar beneath this structure collected all the manure.[29] This was the barn of a progressive farmer. The manure cellar provided the key to scientific farming, as without enough manure fields could not be adequately fertilized. Without adequate fertilization crops would not produce well. Ultimately, livestock would suffer from improper feeding, and their inability to fatten would cost the farmer dearly at the market. In addition, the unfertile fields would not yield a surplus of grains or fodder for the market.

This barn of "ordinary size" and "usual shape" sounds like an English barn, entered and exited on the same long side, about thirty feet from gable to gable, adapted to a progressive farmer's needs. The writer applauded the accommodations for cattle in stables separate from, but adjacent to the main barn. The cellars, too, marked a departure from common practice. This type of barn, the author concluded, built on a plan of about thirty by fifty feet, would obviate the need for multiple barns, a practice that he found still prevailed.

English barns served the needs of small farmers and wealthy landowners alike. In 1831 Benjamin Robinson of Sutton was assessed taxes on fourteen acres, a house and barn. His barn (built around 1806), of ordinary shape and size,

Fig. 19   Robinson barn, c. 1806. Photograph by the author.

measured about thirty-three-and-a-half feet long by twenty feet deep (fig. 19). Its central bay was slightly over fourteen feet wide, its side bays just over nine and ten feet.[30] Lazarus LeBaron's English barn was approximately contemporaneous with Robinson's (fig. 20). LeBaron—merchant, tavern-keeper, and farmer—farmed on a far larger scale than Robinson, and the size of his barn bore witness to that fact. Even so, LeBaron's barn consisted of two barns comparable to Robinson's placed end to end. Only five-and-a-half feet deeper than Robinson's barn, its sixty-three-foot length contained two three-bay barns. LeBaron built bigger, but even he did not incorporate the new-fangled cellars.

LeBaron's bigger barn did not obviate the need for multiple barns. When he died in 1828 his widow, Mary Woodbury LeBaron, received in her dower a portion of the large barn, as well as the garden and close yard with two small barns. These barns all stood near one another on the home lot, cheek by jowl with the LeBaron mansion, all tools in the complex economic interplay of house, yard, and livestock and food storage and processing.

By the 1820s, a new generation of farmers had begun to farm in new ways, due to a variety of economic and social developments, and needed a barn more suited to the modern methods. In 1825 the Worcester Agricultural Society committee examining farms commented with a note of surprise on a barn they saw in Worcester: "What particularly catched our attention, was a new and uncommonly well-built barn, the floor running through it lengthwise. This mode of

Fig. 20 | LeBaron barn. Photograph by the author.

constructing a barn is much preferable to any other, as it gives free access to every part of the barn, by opening a single door."[31] The barn they observed was the New England barn, distinguished from the English barn by its gable-end doors and floor running parallel, rather than perpendicular, to the ridge. Still an uncommon form in Worcester County, the barn had made its appearance in Connecticut River valley towns of Massachusetts by the 1790s. Even in that highly commercialized region, the barns remained rare until the 1840s.[32]

The New England barn seems to have slipped onto the scene quietly, without much fanfare from agricultural improvers who remained close-mouthed about the best manner in which to build a barn into the 1840s. They advised that farmers build a single barn large enough to house the produce of the farm and the cattle, with a cellar for collecting manure, but printed no opinion on whether the new barn form was preferable to the old.[33] Farmers, however, did not hesitate. They took to the new arrangement readily.

Amos Batcheller may have been in the vanguard of Sutton farmers who turned to the New England barn. When Batcheller bought his brother Benjamin's farm in Sutton in 1801 it contained a house, a barn, and a cooper's shop (fig. 21). The house and barn were new, having been built by Benjamin within the previous ten years. The single-story, center-chimney, hall-and-parlor house combined modern and traditional construction techniques, most evident in the roof frame of principal rafters with collar beams, and a five-sided ridgepole.[34] The barn adjoined the northwest corner of the house (fig. 22). Like the house, this four-bay building's roof frame consisted of collared rafters mortised into a five-sided ridgepole. Two open, arched bays on the south side allowed cattle free access to what was probably used only as a cow house. With no evidence that the structure was ever floored, it would have been unsuited to the storage of grains. The fifteen-by-fourteen-foot cooper's shop predated the rest of the buildings on the site, a remnant of the senior Batcheller's mid-eighteenth-century coopering practice.

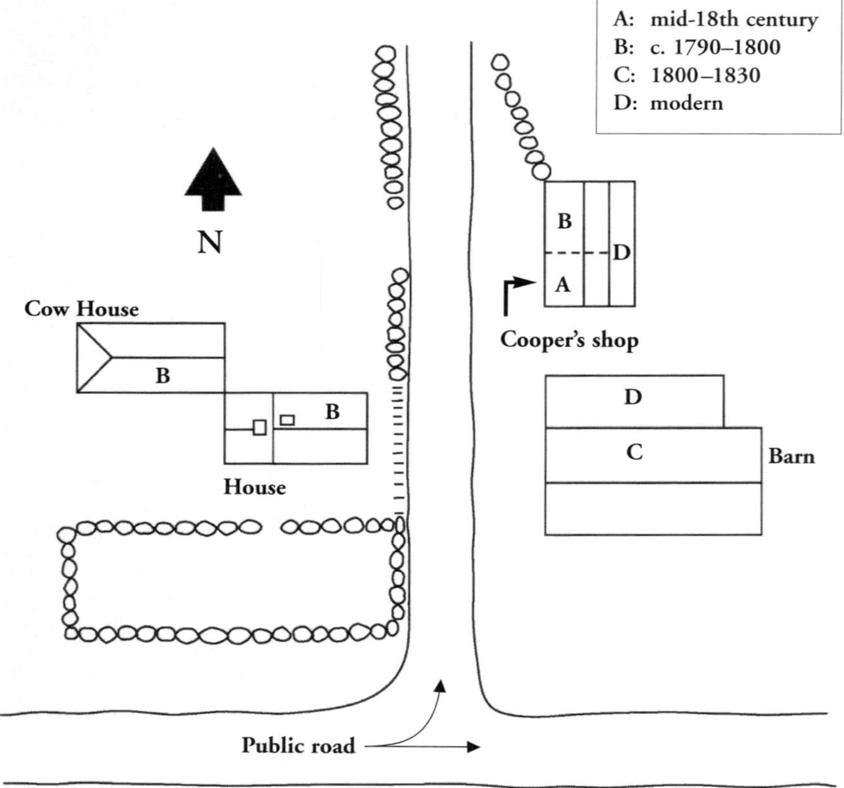

Fig. 21 | Amos Batcheller farmstead, site plan. Drawing by the author.

Fig. 22 Amos Batcheller cow house. Photograph by the author.

To these structures Amos added another barn and enlarged the cooper's shop before his death in 1832. The new Batcheller barn was of ordinary size— approximately thirty feet by thirty-two feet—but not of ordinary configuration. Amos chose to build a three-bay-wide, three-bay-long New England barn with a twelve-foot center drive and side bays of eight-and-a-half feet and ten-and-a-half feet widths (figs. 23, 24). He departed from the agricultural literature by not incorporating cellars, but evidently agreed with agriculturalist and farm journal editor Thomas Fessenden on the siting of the barn. Fessenden advocated locating the barn a convenient distance from the house, and Batcheller built his across the road from his home.[35] Like the house and the older barn, its ridge ran east-west. Unlike those buildings, with entrances on their long north and south sides, one entered this barn on its short east and west gable ends. The siting of the new barn oriented it to the road in front and to the fields behind, rather than to the compass.

The size of Batcheller's operation by 1830 suggests that it was he who doubled the length of his new barn by adding three bents to its west end, illustrating one of the singular advantages of this New England form. In 1830 Amos milked eight cows, double the average for the east side of town where he lived,

Fig. 23   Amos Batcheller's New England barn (foreground) and eighteenth-century cooper's shop (background). Photograph by the author.

and triple the town-wide average.[36] At the time of his death he was down to five cows, but also had three heifers, a calf, a yoke of oxen, a pair of steers, and a horse. He owned a share of a winnowing mill and of a harrow, and possessed three plows. His land holdings totaled 144 acres, again twice the average for his east-side neighbors and three times the town-wide average. As Batcheller's farm operation grew, so could his barn, without any interruption of or change in work patterns, thanks to the parallel drive and roof ridge.

By the early 1830s New England barns were scattered throughout Sutton. Not surprisingly, wealthy and middling farmers accounted for the spate of new barns. In Sutton, the new barn owners' land-holdings ranged from 59 acres to 144 acres, with an average of just over 92.[37] Simeon Stockwell and his neighbors on the west side of town were among those to erect the new barns. Simeon evidently took over running the eighty-acre Holbrook farm when he married Delia Maria Holbrook in 1822, her father having died two years earlier. By 1823 when Simeon and his "honored Mother" Mary Holbrook set aside her dower and entered into a mortgage agreement, two barns stood on the property, one designated old, the other new. The "new" barn stands yet, a New England form with its ridge and drive running east-west and its manure cellar facing south, toward barn yard and road, a conspicuous display of the black gold of cow waste and improved farming if ever there was one.[38]

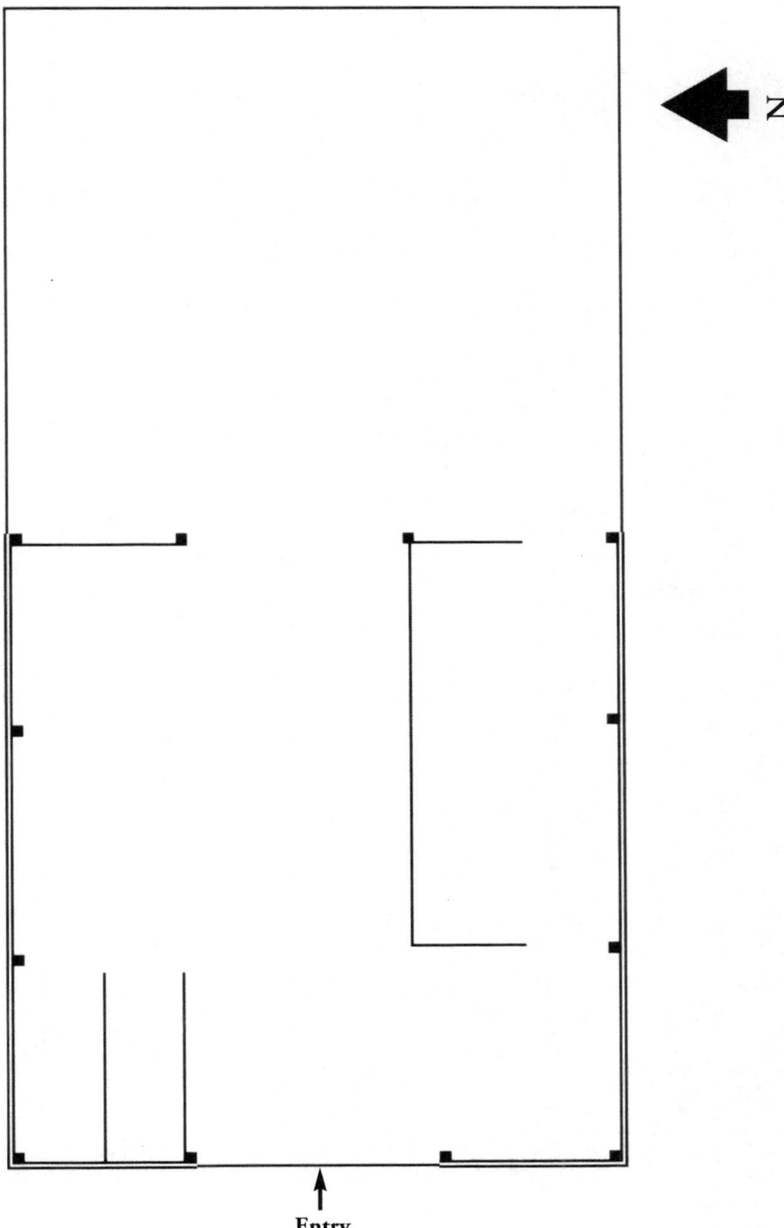

Fig. 24 | Amos Batcheller barn, plan. Drawing by the author.

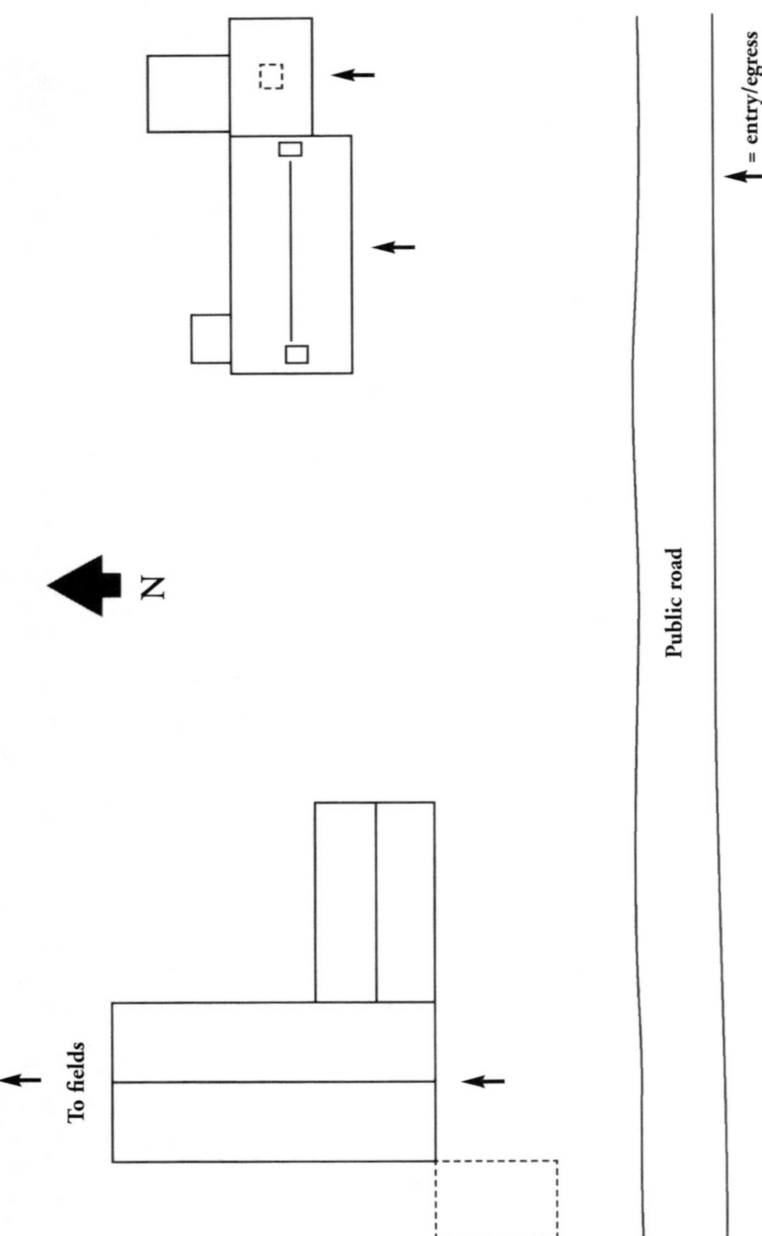

Fig. 25 Stockwell home lot, site plan. Drawing by the author.

In 1830 Enoch Stockwell, his home place lying just west of the Holbrook-Stockwell farm, paid real estate taxes on one house, one barn, two other houses, and ninety acres. His livestock included two oxen, six cows, three young head of cattle, seven sheep, and two hogs. When he died six years later, Stockwell owned even more livestock, having added a horse, a couple more cattle, four more sheep, and several more pigs. With so many animals and acres Stockwell would have needed a large barn, and it seems likely that the New England barn described in his widow's dower stood by 1830.[39]

Stockwell built his barn west of his house, which is dated about 1806, on the same side of the street (fig. 25). The gables of the forty-by-eighty-foot barn faced north and south, toward the fields behind and the road in front. Stabling was to the left of the center drive, mows to the right. Beneath the west (left) bay was a cellar, which, if he followed the agricultural improvers' advice, Stockwell used for collecting manure. Adjacent to the southwest corner of the barn, and attached to it at right angles, was a shed, possibly the chaise house, shed, and wagon house referred to in the widow's dower.

Just to the east of the Stockwell home lots stood the very impressive brick home of John Woodbury. By 1831 Woodbury had transformed a forty-by-thirty-six-foot English barn into a seventy-two-by-forty-foot New England barn complete with cellar (fig. 26).[40] Standing just east of the house, this barn created

Fig. 26 | John Woodbury's New England barn. Photograph by the author.

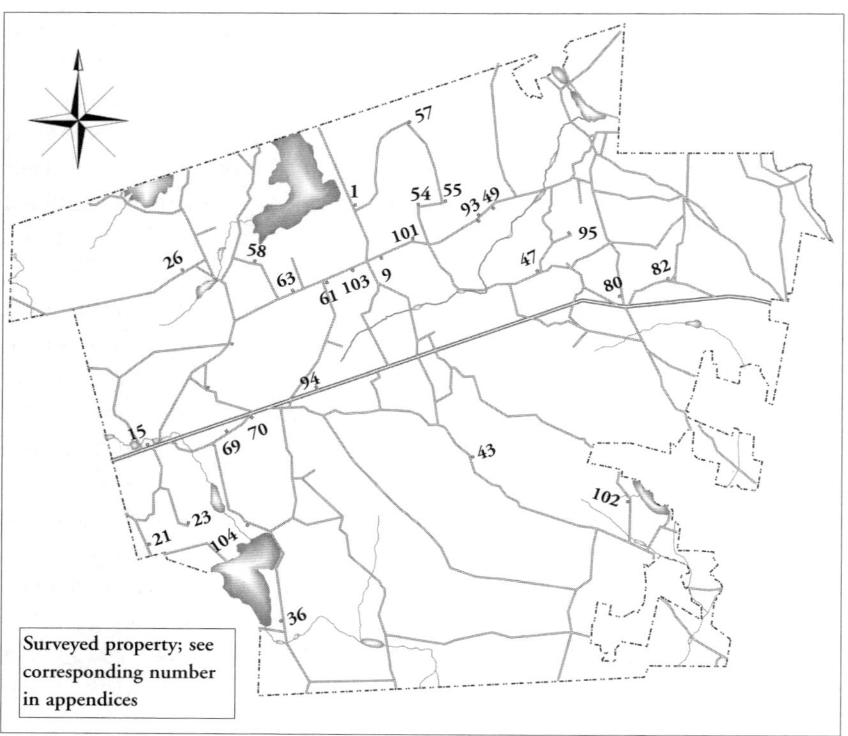

Map 2   Sutton, Massachusetts, showing location of surveyed properties. Surveyed properties with extant barns at the time of survey, c. 1990, include numbers 9, 23, 26, 29, 36, 47, 55, 57, 80, 94, 95. See Appendix A for more detail. Prepared by the author and Rick Riccio.

an even more conspicuous display than its neighbors, with its gable end facing the road to the east and its cellar facing the road to the south (map 2).

The rise in New England barns coincides with an agricultural boom in Sutton in the 1820s. Between 1791 and 1811 the numbers of barns in Sutton varied less than 1 percent. But between 1811 and 1821 barn numbers rose 18 percent and increased by another 22 percent in the next decade. In the 1810s and 1820s farming strategies changed as oats and English hay grew in importance.[41] The total numbers and importance of cows, certainly the primary beneficiaries of better hay and more oats, rose so dramatically that valuators counted them separately from steers and heifers beginning in 1831. The oxen population increased as well. Most people who owned oxen still had only two, indicating that they served as work animals, not as fat cattle. More people kept horses, too, both for pleasure and work. More livestock and more produce added up to the need for more barn space.

The correlation between successful farming and larger barns seems obvious. But larger spaces could have been arranged as Lazarus LeBaron arranged his doubled English barn, or as the 1824 correspondent to the *New England Farmer* recommended. Precisely what distinguished the new barn form from the old? Were those distinguishing characteristics the only factors that determined its preferability, or, as had occurred in the houses, were there underlying shifts in the perceptions of right and proper building for thriving New England farmers?

Sutton's English barns and its New England barns shared some structural characteristics.[42] Barn builders preferred chestnut, hewed major framing members at least into the 1840s, employed the principle rafter/common purlin roof system in both forms, and typically constructed either barn type on a three-bay-wide plan. The widths of the bays did not change dramatically between the two types. The average English barn floor width was eleven feet, while that for New England barns was eleven-and-a-half feet. Both the mow and the stable tended to be just under one foot larger in the New England barn than in the English barn. The dramatic differences between the two barns occurred in the overall square footage, in the frequent construction of cellars in the newer barn form, and in the orientation of the ridge to the floor (fig. 27).

Although the average New England barn stood just two to three feet wider across its entrance façade than the English barn, those that survived into the 1970s had, on average, 900 additional square feet of space. Later barns tended to be larger, however, so we must look at these figures closely. Square footage of surveyed English barns ranged from 506 to 2,124 square feet. New England barn sizes ranged from 1,069 to nearly 2,900 square feet. Sutton farmers therefore built large English barns and small New England barns. Amos Batcheller's New England barn, for example, started out at just under 1,000 square feet, at the small end of the scale for this barn type. Size alone, then, did not determine whether to build an old barn form or a modern one.

The reorientation of the barn floor to a position parallel to the roof ridge brought a new convenience to barn plans. As the Worcester Agricultural Society committee observed in 1825, a single drive gave access to all parts of the barn. English barns enlarged by the addition of extra bays or by the addition of lean-to sheds lacked this convenience. A farmer who added to his English barn had to enter the addition from separate doors or from some corner of the old barn. Cellars, rarely part of the original construction of English barns, became a common, although not inevitable, feature of New England barns,

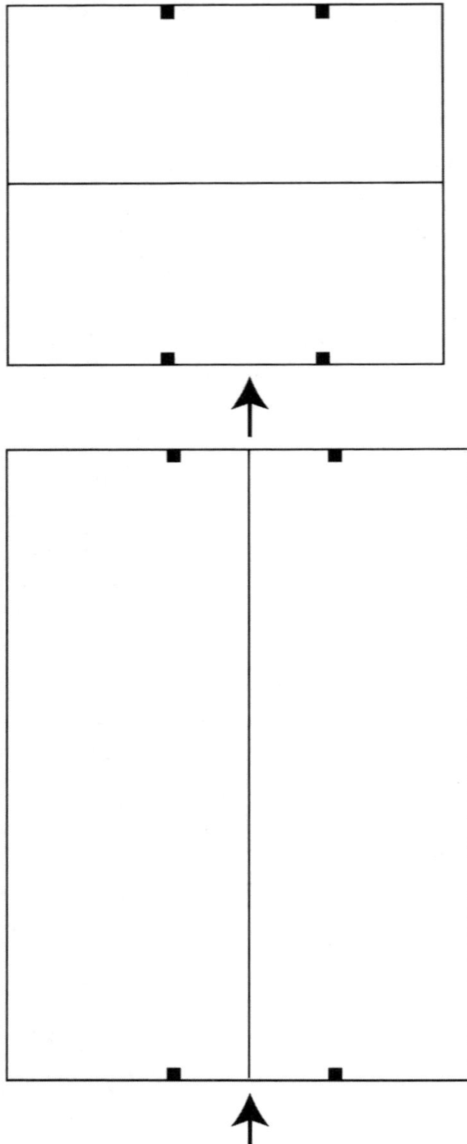

Fig. 27 Comparison of average sizes of English (top) and New England (bottom) barns. Derived from collected data on Sutton barns in Mott and White, *Worcester County Barn Survey, 1976–78,* Old Sturbridge Village Research Dept. files, Sturbridge, Mass. Drawing by the author.

adding to its convenience by increasing the storage space available under a single roof, and by providing a collection area for manure.[43]

Barns, outbuildings, houses, and garden plots clustered within a stone's throw of one another on the house lots that formed the centerpiece of the working farm (fig. 28). Farmers oriented their New England barns toward the house and the fields, accommodating both the women who tended the fowl and milked the cows (at least until dairying became an industry unto itself), and the men who brought in the crops and saw to the feeding and care of livestock. The frequent separation of house from barn by farm roads or public ways should not be viewed as a disuniting factor, but as evidence of the coherent quality of farm production. With house and barn both situated directly on or very near the road, people and products had ready access to the domains of house and barn, as well as to the roads over which goods bound for market were conveyed.

The New England barn met rural householders' demands for convenience and economy. It allowed them to incorporate a proactive efficiency into their daily work patterns, advocated by the newly popular works on domestic and rural economy, reversing the age-old practice of reacting to nature's necessities.[44] Robert B. Thomas's annual *Farmer's Almanac* highlights the change. From 1795 until at least 1804 Thomas's calendar advised turning out young cattle into the woodlands in the spring, shutting up wandering swine in the fall to fatten while turning out shoats at the same time to gather acorns. In the late summer and late fall manure was gathered from wherever it had happened to fall and collected into the barnyard. Agricultural improvers condemned these practices. They advocated that cattle be confined, in part so that their manure, a valuable fertilizer, would not be lost, and that pigs be kept in sties or under barns where they could add to and help process the manure. In January 1799, Thomas acknowledged the tenets of the agricultural improvers while scoffing at their attempts to make farming a scientific enterprise, "Ever desirous that the Farmer's Calendar might be useful to those for whom it is designed, induces the Editor to be attentive in making experiments, and collecting observations from men eminent for improvements in Agriculture. Notwithstanding which, there will appear a sameness in pursuing each month, which is unavoidable while the seasons continue the same."[45]

Beginning around 1806, Thomas's almanac became increasingly preachy and anecdotal and his conversion to agricultural improvement seems complete by 1807. In August of that year he renounced traditional farming practices and the slovenly farms that resulted with this tirade,

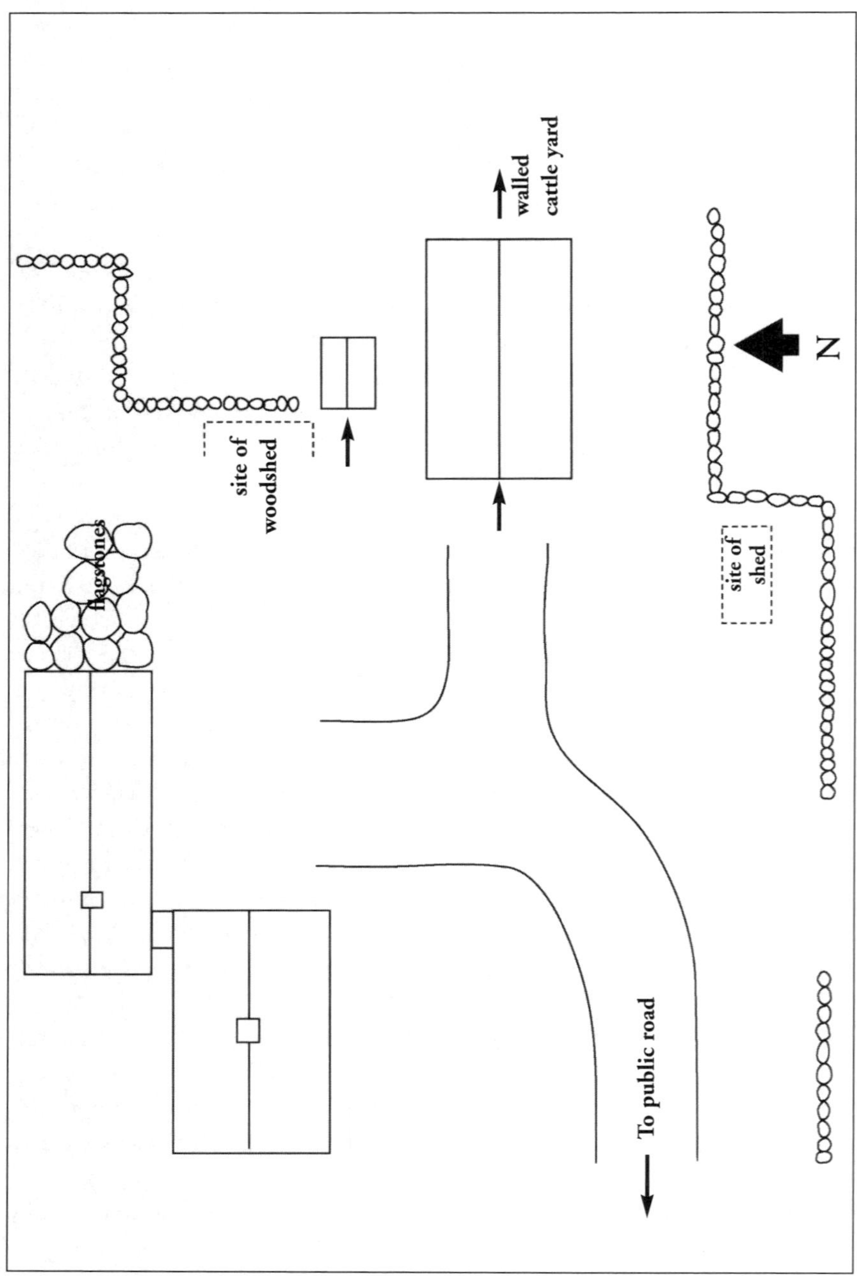

Fig. 28   William Hall farm, homestead site plan. Drawing by the author.

I know many men, who are called farmers, that deserve not the name any more than a cobler does that of a shoemaker. They are such as have inherited from their ancestors large tracts of land called farms, to which they have never added the least kind of improvement; but go on with the same routine of ploughing and sowing, reaping and mowing, every year, as their fathers did before them. Their meadow is made of bulrushes and their upland of brambles. The fences are poor; the barns are shabby; the cattle are lean; the hogs are starved; the houses want new ceiling; and to complete the whole, in many places the master loves new rum and the mistress is a slut![46]

Thomas vividly illustrated the evils of pursuing farming in the old way, while writers of tracts on domestic and rural economy extolled the benefits of improved agriculture. Recall Mr. Smith, the frontier settler in Enos Hitchcock's *The Farmer's Friend,* whom Hitchcock described as "an extensive landholder, and a very respectable farmer." Mr. Smith inspired all who came his way. His house, situated on the southern slope of a hill, "commanded an extensive prospect of well cultivated fields and meadows." His farm buildings were as admirable as his fields. His "large and capacious" barn and granary were "generally filled with the produce of his farm."[47] Through industry Mr. Smith had made his way on the frontier, and his buildings incorporated the convenience and economy that had directed his industry.

Remember, too, Hannah Barnard's cautionary tale of the fate of farm families who lost sight of the virtues of convenience and economy. The debt-ridden Prinks were only saved from destitution by Mrs. Prinks's brother insisting that they sell their fine furnishings and clothing, by his finding a position for Jenny Prinks in the well-run household of Lady Homespun, and by the loan of fifty dollars so Mr. Prinks could build a shed for his cows and a breezeway from the house to the cow shed.[48] Again, as on Mr. Smith's frontier, only through convenience and economy could a farm family hope to sustain itself, and their adoption of those attributes would be visible in the buildings in which they all, men and women, lived and worked. The New England barn answered the need for real and readily apparent convenience and economy. When technological advances in farm equipment proved better suited to the new lands out west, or reformers' programs demanded overhauls of labor systems or farming methods not practicable or desirable to southern New Englanders, the new barn presented a visible reminder that the New England farmer was as wide awake as those in supposedly less hide-bound occupations. It served as both evidence of, and tool for, financial success.

The entrenchment of large-scale factories on the landscape and in the economy coincided with the new agricultural directions of the 1820s. Jonathan Prude in his study of Douglas and Oxford, just south of Sutton, argued that the economic shifts that occurred in those towns, and throughout much of rural New England in the early nineteenth century, were not simply attributable to the arrival of industry, but rather to the interplay of manufacturing and agricultural interests.[49] In similar fashion, the interplay of manufacturing and farming accounts for the physical transformation of the rural Blackstone River valley between 1820 and 1840.

Over the course of the first four decades of the nineteenth century, farming became increasingly specialized not only in the items produced, but in the population producing them. In other words, a higher percentage of the population became divorced from farm pursuits, meaning that in Sutton, fewer farmers provided slightly more produce on slightly more land. As more people found themselves removed from farming, both raw and finished agricultural products became more marketable. The trend can be seen in Sutton where in 1820 16 percent of the total population was involved in farming, while only a quarter of that amount, 4.5 percent, was involved in manufacturing. Ten years later the numbers changed dramatically. Of the total population in Sutton, only 10 percent was counted as farmers, while 11 percent was employed in factory production.[50]

While the scale of Sutton's agricultural landscape did not change in the first forty years of the nineteenth century, it joined with much of the rest of the Blackstone River valley in those years in changing the scale and scope of its manufacturing, in creating what has since been labeled the industrial revolution. With only half of its total acreage devoted to agriculture in the early national period, Sutton had plenty of room to accommodate larger mills and manufacturing complexes. In the 1820s and 1830s investors developed new water privileges and enlarged several sites already occupied by various types of mills. The largest manufacturing interests developed in the northeast corner of Sutton, along the Blackstone River (supplemented by the Blackstone Canal in 1828) and Cold Spring Brook, and in the southwest along the Mumford River and around Manchaug Pond, while smaller operations continued to operate on all water privileges (map 3). By 1830 Sutton's manufacturing enterprises ranged from company-owned villages to small manufacturing enclaves to dozens of small shops scattered throughout town. Wilkinsonville on the Blackstone River and Manchaug village on the Mumford River contained the largest manufacturing establishments, but manufacturing extended

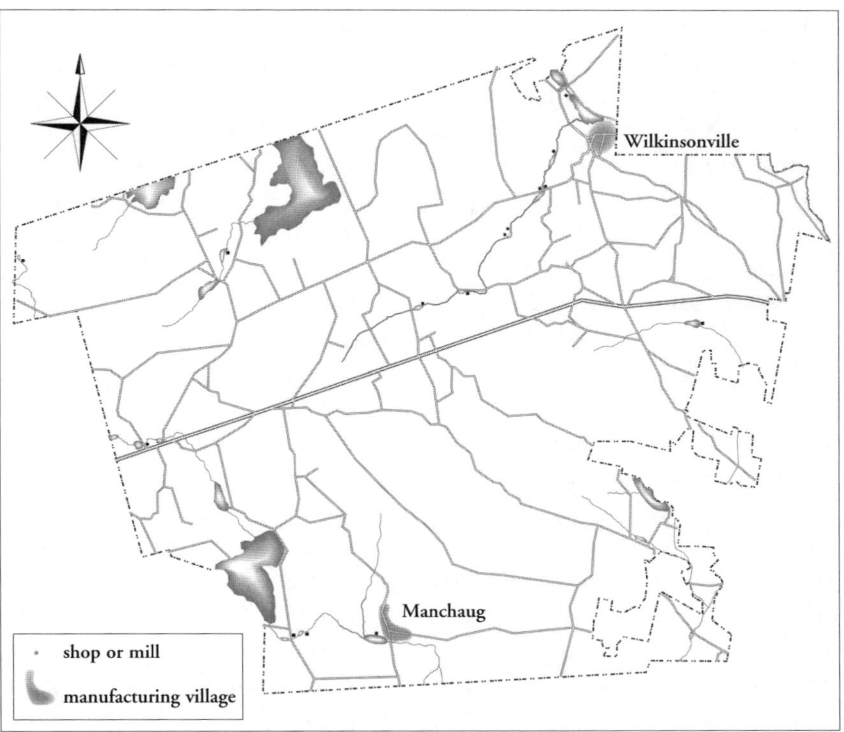

Map 3 | Sutton, Massachusetts, showing locations of mills and manufacturing villages present by 1830. Water-powered mills and manufacturing villages dotted all of Sutton's major waterways by 1830. Dozens of small shops were scattered throughout town. Prepared by the author and Rick Riccio.

well beyond those sites. Scores of smaller shops emerged, run by local farmers, artisans, and mechanics.

Already renowned at the end of the eighteenth century for its "manufactures, its mills, and water works," in the next four decades Sutton further exploited its waterways, and its natural and human resources, to increase production of goods for sale.[51] The expansion of the manufacturing landscape had little impact on farmlands, but significantly altered the town's wetlands. With three large ponds, the Blackstone River, and numerous smaller streams and wetlands, Sutton never suffered from a shortage of water. Its streams provided several excellent natural mill sites. In the early decades of the nineteenth century Sutton residents increased the productivity of their groundwater by redirecting, damming, and ponding it. In the final calculation, the town's total acreage under water increased from 1 percent to just over 4 percent. While agricultural lands held steady, or gained slightly in the early nineteenth century, lands classified as unimproved or unimprovable, often marsh or swamp areas, fell off markedly between 1811 and 1841. In 1811, the first year with data that can be considered reliable for wastelands, unimproved and unimprovable acres occupied 44 percent of Sutton's lands. Thirty years later, less than 20 percent of Sutton was classified as wasteland. While some of that can be attributed to farmers' reclamation of "waste," increased amounts of land devoted to manufacturing accounts for most of the drop in unimproved acreage.

Many of the improvements to water privileges in this post-revolutionary era required no sharp departure from longstanding practices, only a change in scale. Scythe production offers one example of the continuities between an economy and landscape dominated by agriculture, and an economy and landscape shared by manufacturing and farming interests. Blacksmiths probably produced scythes for most of the eighteenth century in the vicinity of West Sutton, along the Mumford River as it entered and left Manchaug Pond, and on the water privileges to the north of Singletary Pond, but the early history of these shops is still vague.[52] By 1793 Sutton supported five scythe and axe shops and seven triphammer shops. Some of the blacksmith owners of those triphammer shops—water powered and horse powered—used them to turn out scythes and axes by the 1780s.[53]

The nature of scythe manufacturing in Sutton seems to have changed in the 1810s. In 1813 four local men established a scythe manufactory along Cold Spring Brook. The number of investors suggests that this was to be a larger-scale operation than the older blacksmith-owned and -operated shops. These men sold out within a couple of years to Captain Asa Woodbury, also of Sutton. Woodbury set about to improve the site, and by 1833 he owned at least two houses, a scythe and spindle shop with water-powered triphammer, and a woolen mill, all along the banks of Cold Spring Brook. One of Woodbury's houses was the "Company's House," and very likely housed the six adult males he employed in the scythe and spindle shop.[54] In this way, Woodbury not only supplied the growing textile factories with spindles, but continued to serve farmers by producing the venerable scythe.

All told, Sutton's three major scythe manufacturers shipped out over 13,000 scythes in 1833 to dealers in Massachusetts, Maine and New York. The scope of these operations had broadened from pre-revolutionary times, but some aspects of this work fell well within longstanding practices. Unlike textile mills, with their dozens of laborers, the scythe shops employed between four and six young men over age sixteen. The work evidently continued to require some level of skill, for they all received between twenty-five and fifty cents more per day than their counterparts in the local cotton mills. In a pattern of work familiar to all "pre-industrial" workers, the shop owners employed their help only eight to ten months out of the year.[55]

That work pattern in water-powered operations had always been due to both the seasonal flow of water and to the rhythms of farm work. Lewis Torrey and David Dudley, both relying on water-powered triphammers in their shops, continued to operate in this farmer/artisan mode. Lewis Torrey, remembered in the 1878 Sutton history only as a blacksmith with a small shop in the Manchaug district, produced 3,600 scythes a year. Torrey's real estate consisted of a house, shop, barn, and sixty-six acres. In the 1830s Torrey owned two oxen, which provided the means of planting at least some of his acreage; two to four cows, the produce from which may have been used only to feed his large family (thirteen children by 1839); and a horse. He also kept a hog each year for butchering. In 1835, Torrey's profits enabled him to loan out $400 at interest. David Dudley followed a very similar strategy. He maintained two houses, two shops, a barn, and forty-six acres. He, too, prepared fields with two oxen and kept four cows, a horse or two, and a hog. With his children ranging between the ages of twenty-six and thirteen by 1830, the milk from the Dudley's four cows may have been used by Mrs. Dudley and her adolescent daughter to produce saleable butter and cheeses.[56]

Like their counterparts in previous generations, Torrey and Dudley continued to pursue a number of means of maintaining their households. The rhetorical division between farmers and mechanics, or farmers and artisans, played up by so many of the early republic's politicians and popular speakers, would not have been recognized by these men and their families. Farming remained an important part of their economic strategies, as did production of agricultural implements. Pushed, perhaps, by the disruptions in trade brought about by the military conflict between France and England and by the War of 1812, these artisans created larger and more efficient triphammer shops that allowed them to supply the growing regional markets, and on a scale that earned them the title of manufacturer rather than smithy.

The mill villages that developed throughout the Blackstone River valley in the generation after the War for Independence far outstripped enterprises like those of Dudley and Torrey in terms of capital invested and capital improvement, but they developed alongside those operations, neither replacing them nor prompting their existence. The industrialization of the countryside did not occur because the larger manufacturers moved in, but because of broader demographic and economic developments in which everyone participated, albeit on unequal footing in some cases. Sutton's company-owned mill villages, while controlled by outside investors, do not seem to have pre-empted local initiative, nor were they entirely without local associations.

The earlier of the two major company villages in Sutton grew along water privileges on the Blackstone River in the northeast corner of town. While Asa Woodbury developed his water privileges with his scythe, spindle, and wool operations, Elijah Waters and Asa Waters Jr. of the newly incorporated town of Millbury, gained control of water privileges along the Blackstone River.[57] In Sutton, Asa Waters acquired a site known as the Dudley farm in 1815 and built a dam, a sawmill, a gristmill, and a small cotton yarn factory. The yarn mill burned in 1822 and Waters sold the entire site to David Wilkinson of North Providence, Rhode Island, in 1823. Wilkinson promptly built a stone factory in which he manufactured cotton thread. Between 1823 and 1829 he developed the site extensively, enlarging the factory, constructing a hotel, an Episcopal church, a bank, and several dwellings for the company's employees.[58]

Local men served as agents or superintendents of the Wilkinson mills for at least part of the village's early history. The nature of the relationships between the absentee owner and his supervisors remains unclear at this point, but some tantalizing evidence suggests at least a high level of regard for Wilkinson, if not a personal relationship. Deacon John Morse, a tanner, descendent of Morses who arrived in town in 1734, and a man of some standing in his own right in the community, served as the agent for Waters's yarn mill. He may have continued in that capacity for Wilkinson, for the Morses named their last son, born in 1825, for the mill owner. Morse is lost to the local records before 1830, when the assessor began to keep detailed records of personal and real property, but the house he built on the Boston Post Road east of the town center between 1811 and 1815 still stands. Like many of his contemporaries Morse built a two-story, center-hall house with an integral rear ell. Finished with the delicate detailing of Federal-era neoclassicism, the Morse house displayed a level of taste expected of genteel folk, as well as a thoroughly modern concern for convenience. All of this added up to a statement of independence and stature, suggesting that the mill owner's agent did not consider himself subordinate to his employer.

Joshua Armsby Jr., a machinist and carpenter, also served as superintendent for the Wilkinson mills for several years. A man of considerable personal property, Armsby served as representative to the Massachusetts General Court for four years in the 1830s, and established his own machine shop in 1835. Armsby, who built a large two-story, double-pile house with side ell around the time of his second marriage in 1823, evidently farmed with the same intensity he pursued mechanical interests. By 1830 he owned 93 acres of land, two oxen, four cows, two hogs, and one pleasure horse. In 1839 he built a modern New England barn, and by 1841 he owned three more head of cattle and thirty more acres. Armsby continued to accumulate more land and more livestock for at least the next ten years.[59]

For men like Morse and Armsby, the industrialization of their rural neighborhoods brought increased opportunity. Neither Morse nor Armsby depended upon the Wilkinsonville mills for their livings. Unlike the sixty women and girls who earned forty cents a day, or the dozen boys under sixteen years old who earned thirty cents a day, or the twenty men who earned a dollar a day, Armsby and Morse commanded other sorts of capital—including cash, credit, real or personal estate—that they could put to work for them. With the coming of larger-scale industries, they could cash in as well on their artisanal or mechanical skills.

The growth of cotton mills such as those at Wilkinsonville and the even larger operation in Manchaug afforded still other opportunities for the mechanics of the Blackstone River valley, including supplying the demand for shuttles. As had been the case with scythe manufacturing, the industrialized production of shuttles fit into established patterns of work. By the early 1830s, Sutton had three shuttle manufacturers, all of whom seemed to operate on the same scale as the scythe makers. As at the scythe shops, the four to six employees at each shop worked only ten months out of the year and earned twenty-five cents more per day than their counterparts in the mills. This work could be either water- or horse-powered. Milton Ruggles built his shuttle shop on an eighteenth-century grist and sawmill site north of Wilkinsonville, at Pleasant Falls, in 1832.[60] Joseph Hathaway produced shuttles at his horse-powered machine shop in the early 1830s, apparently at the same time he operated a sawmill, but sold out before 1835 to Ezra S. Marble.[61] Marble's modest endeavor gradually grew into a family manufacturing enclave known as Marbleville. Through the construction of reservoirs and dams, Marble turned his entire operation into one powered by water.[62]

Like his counterparts in scythe-making, shuttle-maker Origen Harback pursued both farming and manufacturing. Married before 1817, Origen controlled a good amount of capital by the time his last child was born in 1824. In 1830, the earliest enumeration of personal and real property available, Harback owned a house, a barn, a shop, fifty acres, a chaise, four cows, two other head of cattle, a pleasure horse, and two hogs. Throughout the 1830s and 1840s Harback kept between four and seven head of cattle of various kinds, a horse or two, and at least one hog. His land holdings never fell below fifty acres. For at least fifteen years, Harback operated two shops. When Samuel Ward observed Harback's shuttle operation in the early 1830s, he pronounced its machinery "the most ingenious and useful of any that has come under my examination. The wood work of the shuttle, after it is blocked out, is entirely completed by the operation of machinery, for the reception of irons."[63] Harback successfully negotiated the mixed agricultural and manufacturing economy of the early nineteenth century using already well-established models. His own great-uncle had established a carding and fulling mill in Sutton around 1776, and his cousin, Thomas Harback Jr. had built a woolen broadcloth mill with power looms in 1822. Even with new endeavors such as the large-scale manufacture of shuttles, then, old patterns of achieving or ensuring competencies persisted.

While Torrey, Dudley and Harback all represent the successful integration of agricultural and manufacturing pursuits, they were also among the few who could afford such capital-intensive ventures. In industrializing southeastern Massachusetts, farmers, artisans, mechanics, and their wives and children combined agriculture with handcraft work at a level not worthy of note in the Secretary of the Treasury's 1833 census of manufacturing, but well worth noting here. The participation of farm families in a newly diversified agricultural and manufacturing economy manifested itself in the landscape, as families rebuilt and rearranged their homes and homesteads, and as they added increasing numbers of shops to their holdings.[64]

Sutton's shops boomed in the 1810s, prior to the establishment of local large-scale textile mills, but simultaneously with the rise of textile mills throughout the Blackstone River valley.[65] A shop consisted of an operation such as blacksmithing, coopering, wheel-wrighting, cabinet-making, carriage-building, fancy painting, or shoe making. The Worcester County Decennial Valuation for 1801–31 lists these as "shops within or adjoining to dwelling houses," and as "other shops." They were counted separately from all types of factories and mills. Sutton started the new century with a total of thirty shops. In 1831, Sutton and Millbury together (Millbury having been separated from Sutton in 1813) contained 101 shops, with over half of those being in Sutton. Worcester, at the headwaters of the Blackstone River just north of Millbury, showed comparable growth. That town had only eighteen shops in 1801. The number increased sevenfold by 1831 to 124. Throughout the Blackstone River valley, the story was the same.[66]

If we define a farmer as an individual with reported land and livestock holdings on the Sutton town valuations and tax lists, then farmers owned 85 percent of the shops standing in town in 1830, and 76 percent in 1841. The definition is broad, but it eliminates everyone who was completely divorced from agriculture. The property holdings of these shop-owning farmers ranged from 4 acres to 265, the median holding being 45 acres and the average 67, comparable to the town-wide average of 58 acres. Their livestock holdings ranged from one cow to forty-six animals, with everyone owning at least one cow. Shop owners held an average of 3.75 cows each, an increase of one animal over the town-wide average.[67]

The fact that the smallest landholder in that shop-owner group, Amos Armsby, owned seven animals, the median holding for this group, indicates that there were numerous strategies for succeeding in this new economy of the early nineteenth century. Armsby was a carpenter and machinist, his large shop operated by horsepower.[68] Unlike many of his horse-owning townsmen and nearly half of the shop owners, he did not own a chaise.[69] He evidently used his animals strictly for work. His two oxen and two cows may have provided a source of income also, as he could have hired out the oxen to plow fields and sold any surplus milk products from the cows. Armsby's four acres would not have supported all of his animals. He either boarded his animals, bought feed, or rented pasture. Sutton farmers like Armsby were not simply producing more agricultural products for the new markets created by the industrialization of the Blackstone valley, they were creating those markets and contributing to the growth of manufactures.

William Hall, farmer, housewright, and millwright, was among those individuals who contributed to the rise of shops in the 1810s. While the forms of Armsby's house, barn and shop remain a mystery, William Hall's homestead still stands (fig. 29). Hall returned home to Sutton from Warwick, Rhode Island, around 1811. Assuming possession of the old family farm, he made many improvements, including a house ell that contained his workshop, and a New England barn. An enclosed breezeway connected the ell to the northeast corner of the house. The west end of the ell contained a chimney stack with set kettle. Hall's enormous work table stood against the north wall. The

Fig. 29 William Hall's New England barn, with house ell visible in the background. Photograph by the author.

workshop extended beyond the east end of the ell, onto a flagstoned area. An open woodshed, its ridge at right angles to the ridge of the ell, projected from the front right corner of the ell, completing the work area. With the house, these structures formed a small courtyard.[70]

To the east and south of these buildings stood the farm structures, their roof ridges all parallel to those of the house and ell. The cellarless New England barn, itself a sign of modernized farming practices, could be entered from the fields to the east, or from the drive to the west. One small shed remains to the left of the barn, another stood southwest of the barn. These buildings formed the east side of a large yard or courtyard. The house and ell defined the north side, and a stone wall enclosed the south side. Within this courtyard, male and female farm and manufacturing activities would have mixed freely, the women passing back and forth between the barn and house as they carried on the dairying, the men's daily activities taking them between field, barn and ell. Like his counterparts in scythe and shuttle production, Hall employed extra hands. Four male laborers lived with the Halls in 1820. The census taker in that year recorded only one individual engaged in agriculture, which may or may not mean that the laborers only assisted Hall in his shop. In 1830 the Halls had only two extra male hands.

Hall's 1859 inventory of his estate paints a portrait of an active farmer. His livestock included a horse, a pair of oxen, ten other head of cattle, pigs, and fowls. His farm tools included three grain cradles, a cultivator, and three plows. But he also still owned his woodworking tools, among which were a cross-cut saw, two wood saws, three axes, chisels, an adze, a try square, and several chests of unenumerated tools. Hall's real and personal estate indicates that he was equipped to pursue two occupations. In the larger scheme of things, Hall and his wife made only modest alterations to the landscape, but those alterations enabled them to accommodate their multiple roles and occupations in the mixed agricultural and manufacturing economy.

These farmers supplied not only local storekeepers, but extra-local markets with butter, cheese, shoes, combs, tools, plows, furniture, and more. When Benedict and Tracy wrote in 1878 of the "certain returns of honest industry upon the farm," they may have had these industrious farmers in mind—the people of their grandparents' generation whose time-softened stories and reminiscences of farm life prior to the disruptions of the Civil War may indeed have sounded like a golden age.[71] But it was a farm life inextricably bound up with manufacturing and industrialization, a connection that Benedict and Tracy chose not to explore. Instead, they observed that manufacturing grew in Sutton as a result of English oppression, which inspired every household to become a "manufactory of cloth." The authors credited farmers only with the production of wool and flax to support that home production.[72] The farmers went well beyond such production, of course, and in the process created a farmscape that served not only economic needs, but also cultural expectations for order and economy of effort. Fences and stone walls neatly delineated fields and yards, carefully separating pasture from hay field and hay field from cultivated field, as well as home lot from farm fields. New barns could grow incrementally and never break the ridgeline, never disturb the linear flow of work reminiscent of the new factory system. Independent shops contained tools of a non-farm trade, still conducted on the homeplace, but appropriately occupying their own spaces. No doubt these very busy places would appear disheveled, if not downright chaotic, to our eyes. But there was a logic to the pattern the farmers created; a logic lost over the years as observers and critics lost sight of the vitality of this countryside, and of its economic realities, replacing the productive working nature of farm life with bucolic or pastoral imagery.

Conclusion

The propensity for two-story dwellings where single-stories had dominated for a century or more was disturbing to many observers, but not surprising given the rejuvenation of the economy and the rapid industrialization of many rural districts in New England. The availability of cash and credit enabled many rural inhabitants to build or rebuild houses and farmsteads, while new demands on space and time required that they do so with economy and convenience in mind. But the temporal coincidence of money and new building forms does not necessarily imply causal relationships. Money permitted, and work and living requirements demanded a new order, but popular perceptions of beauty and convenience actually shaped the reordering of the post-Revolution rural New England landscape.

In the early nineteenth century, reformers equated order and convenience with industry and productivity. Neat—that is, well-ordered—fields, fences, yards, and houses signaled sound morals and prosperity to contemporary observers. When Timothy Dwight published his 1790s travels in the early 1810s, he repeatedly equated neat and tidy landscapes and buildings with morally upstanding inhabitants. Except for the laborers, the inhabitants of New Haven, Connecticut, were all, according to Dwight, "industrious and thriving," their buildings "neat and tidy." Worcester's buildings were nearly uniformly neat and tasteful. The houses and farms of Princeton, Massachusetts, suggested prosperity to Dwight who declared the inhabitants unequivocally industrious, sober, and of sound morals.[1]

Agricultural journals echoed and amplified Dwight's sentiments. They declared neatness and order to be necessary characteristics of respectability. The *New England Farmer* went beyond its 1827 equation of a farmer's and farmwife's character with the appearance of their dooryard when the editor asserted in 1829 that neatness was essential to both health and respectability, its lack both extravagant and disgraceful.[2]

Order and convenience, then, were not only evidence of and necessary components of good character, but also of economy. Visible evidence of economy demonstrated the absence of extravagance and non-republican luxury. Economy in farming and domestic practices implied industriousness. It implied that the farm family wasted nothing—not land, not bread, not time. Attached house ells with indoor wells, a chimney stack with oven and set kettle, indoor wood storage, and even a privy in some cases, made everyone's life somewhat easier, but notably economized women's labor. The new barn form, with its drive parallel to its ridge, epitomized economy. The reordered barns could not only accommodate more animals and larger crops, they made tending to livestock and storing grain more efficient. At a time when order and convenience signaled moral rectitude, the New England barn was not just a practical accommodation to new spatial needs, it served also as a monument to a farmer's success, modernity, and good character.

To the builders and architects of the Age of Improvement, classicism was the only architectural vocabulary appropriate to the new republic. Beauty, in popular culture, was an absolute quality. In architecture, the Greek and Roman orders were seen as the attainment of perfection. Not yet privy to picturesque theory, which would be popularized with Andrew Jackson Downing's publications in the 1840s, and still immersed in the Enlightenment fascination with antiquity, most people were not ready to accept the notion of rural beauty as dependent on a natural quality that rural reformers promoted in the 1820s. The Georgian ideal, with its symmetry and implied distinctions in room functions, had been long in coming to the middling ranks and refused to be dislodged.

It seems that only with the confluence of revolutionary fervor for independence with the post-revolutionary fervor for equality and improvement were conditions right for the new manifestation of beauty and convenience as classical detail, Georgian symmetry, and modern order. As the centerpiece of the nation's economy and the foundation of its government, reformers told farmers, the free and independent yeoman had a right as well as a duty to improve himself and his environment. Middling ranks of rural inhabitants, eager to conform to contemporary and popular standards of propriety, proceeded to do just that. In their domestic arrangements, however, they chose a form that did not fit the reforming gentry's notion of proper rural housing.

The order, symmetry, and style of the new houses, and of the remodeled old ones, marked their owners as citizens, even as gentry, of the new national order. Beauty was inherent in the houses' two-story height and classical detail; convenience evident in their ells. Such forms implied modernity and an improving mentality. This is not to say that farmers reordered their land as a symbolic gesture, or because they owed it to their nation. Rather, new demographic trends and market opportunities required more land under more intensive cultivation, more intensive use of men's and women's labor and time, which in turn required reordered farms and homes. As they rebuilt, these farmers adopted the new aesthetic of beauty and convenience that not only suited their practical needs, but also demonstrated their sound morals and good taste. Here an interesting question arises, for the ell houses gained currency in urban areas at the same time. One wonders to what extent and how rapidly urban artisans actually did separate their workspaces from their homes as they are supposed to have done in the first decades of the nineteenth century, and how artisans' wives utilized both the space and their time. While the construction of separate artisanal or merchant shops has been documented, the actual patterns of use of the new houses by the women at home remains unclear. To what extent did the houses respond to a need for the women to continue or to intensify their contribution to household finances in an era of economic upheaval?[3]

For all its modern attributes, early-nineteenth-century rural New England housing evolved from and continued to use traditional building practices. Rural builders based house plans on center-chimney or center-hall arrangements that had been in circulation since initial settlement in the colony in the first case, and for over a century in the second. While some builders experimented with new framing methods, post-and-beam frames remained common practice into the last quarter of the nineteenth century. Patterns of room use did not change immediately either. The presence of ells and two stories did not, as we have seen, mean an assumption of urban or elite separation of service and social functions, nor did it imply the luxury of reserving rooms for a single or occasional use. On the contrary, multiple function rooms and mixed social and service areas persisted.

The ostensibly innovative rural dwellers who built the two-story-with-ell houses were actually maintaining common or traditional building practices as well as continuity in local society. Those who undertook the building campaigns in Sutton were well established. Born in Sutton and surrounding communities for the most part, they had extensive kin networks. In their building campaigns they retained familiar social and architectural structures while employing a recently popularized aesthetic.

The reordered rural landscape suggests that thriving New England farmers were ordering their lives and environments along sound moral and practical principles. The classically detailed two-story-with-ell houses, the aligned barns and the tidy yards and fields fulfilled demands for beauty and convenience. But the agricultural press and rural reformers complained of extravagance, luxury, and the loss of rural virtues such as self-sacrifice, independence, and simplicity, all of which stemmed from the proclivity for two-story houses. The form and plans of the two-story dwellings that proliferated in the countryside in the early nineteenth century were based on longstanding practices, but their numbers, their non-incremental construction, their increasingly prominent classical detail, and their ells were new. To those reformers alarmed by developments in New England's rural architecture, those discontinuities with past experience defined the rebuilding they observed in the hinterland.

Farming, housing and improvement all had different meanings for different groups of people. The traditional Yankee elite could not look at the countryside without seeing the fate of the nation in the balance, and because their definitions of those concepts varied from the definitions held by farmers, the reformers could only construe what they saw as negative. They imbued agrarianism with the significance of antiquity and heralded it as the crux of the national economy. In the early nineteenth century reformers regularly berated farmers for not employing more scientific agricultural practices, or gently chided them for not being awakened to the possibilities of modern farming, for being "more quiet, less adventurous, and less active" than non-farmers.[4] Simultaneously, in keeping with classical and biblical writings, the agricultural improvers and rural reformers acknowledged farmers as the moral inferiors of no one. Retaining their virtuous status required that the yeomanry retain those qualities for which the great Roman republics were noted—namely self-sacrifice, independence, and simplicity. Rural reformers did not see working farmers cultivating any of those qualities on their improved farmsteads.

Reformers saw small houses and small, productive farms as the key to keeping farmers within their social station and to maintaining the virtues inherent in rural, specifically farm, life. They countered the new two-story landscape with their own rustic visions of country life. The reformers' idea of an appropriate rural landscape was one dominated by quaint, simple dwellings ornamented by nature and nestled discretely among well-ordered yards and prosperous fields, a distinctly non-materialistic image. This vision contrasted directly with the classical vocabulary popular with the middling and upper ranks of society. Furthermore, it directly contradicted the advice given to rural builders in architectural handbooks and builder's guides for improving the appearance of the new nation.

The manifestation of taste seen in the rise of classical detail on rural dwellings disturbed New England's reformers. It was an incursion into what had been, hitherto, the province of well-educated gentry. To the traditional gentry the appropriation by the common folk of genteel ornament symbolized the decay of the old order. In it they saw the vices of luxury, extravagance, and debt, any and all of which meant the downfall of republican society and virtue. Without the sturdy and simple yeoman to serve as the pillar of society, a nation could not thrive. To be free and independent farmers needed to be free of debt, guided by their common sense rather than by external forces of markets or creditors. To be tempted by luxury, as most common folk seemed to be, was to lose sight of the self-sacrifice and simplicity required of republican yeomen.

The *New England Farmer's* assessment that "a firm and independent spirit is better nourished among that rank of men, by whom small farms are cultivated" and that "their simple virtues will give its character to a country, and uphold in the hour of danger, the rights and liberties of all" was popular rhetoric.[5] The agricultural press and the speeches and writings of rural reformers repeated variations on that theme for decades. To the wealthy reformers, independence meant freedom from debt, hence the cry for small houses and small farms. Economy demanded simplicity in material life, hence the promotion of the beauties of natural ornament over the indulgence of classical decorations. To the farmers, independence more likely came with the amount of credit one commanded. Debt was a fact of life in a financial network where little currency exchanged hands and where accounts were settled periodically rather than as each transaction took place. Reformers and farmers each interpreted "economy" quite differently. To farmers, economy demanded convenience and order, not stark simplicity or a disavowal of all consumer goods.

The post-Revolution middling and upper-class Yankee perceptions of classicism and improvement, of beauty and convenience, faded away in the 1840s. The idea that an individual had a right and duty to improve himself or herself and his or her surroundings continued into the next era, however, taking on a life of its own, even as republican virtue faded from national discussion. In its new garb, the patriotic duty to improve became the duty to consume, so that in 1868 Reverend Henry Ward Beecher could write, "Whatever expenditure refines the family and lifts it into a larger sphere of living, is really spent upon the whole community as well. . . . A community needs examples to excite its ambition. A noble dwelling is, in part, the property of all who dwell near it.

Fine grounds not only confer pleasure directly on all who visit or pass by, but they excite every man of any spirit to improve his own grounds."[6] The traditional communities intolerant of open-ended consumption were clearly a thing of the past in Beecher's rural New England.

The architectural critics of the antebellum years were thoroughly taken with the new picturesque aesthetic. For Andrew Jackson Downing and other popularizers of the picturesque in the 1840s and 1850s, there was no longer a "true style." Roman, Italian, and "rural Gothic" styles were all preferable to pure Greek or pure Gothic for rural domestic buildings. Styles were adapted to particular situations and uses. The belief in a universal classical aesthetic was dead. These critics often dealt harshly with the revolutionary and republican generation's classicism. In 1847 William Ranlett condemned Vitruvius, Palladio, and Serlio, and noted that, "It is an imbecility of our nature, to venerate and lean upon hoary antiquity, when better guides are at hand." In discussing the English cottage style he observed "[t]he improved taste of modern times, has repudiated the monotony of regular houses . . . so common in the several classical styles, in the favor bestowed upon the several modifications of the Gothic." Even while Charles Dickens was commenting on the brilliance of the seemingly new white buildings of Worcester, more in a tone of amazement than of condemnation, Ranlett was condemning the "dazzling white" of wooden buildings as being in "decidedly bad taste."[7] The white of the ancient Greek ruins was not expressive or evocative, qualities required of colors in the picturesque era, it was only intrusive.

Just as the disapproval of early-nineteenth-century agricultural improvers and rural reformers had not dissuaded rural residents from building their large, classically detailed dwellings, the scorn of the new generation of reformers for classicism, straight lines, and symmetry failed to dislodge the form from rural builders' repertoires. Sutton farmers continued to build two-story, single- and double-pile farmhouses with side or rear ells into the 1870s that looked very much like their 1820s and 1830s counterparts. Although the meaning with which the New England landscape had been imbued by a generation steeped in classical republicanism and democracy was lost, the forms persisted, invested, no doubt, with a new set of values.

Seeing farmers as the inheritors of classical rural virtues, reformers could only be appalled at the perceived luxury and profligacy of that caste. Envisioning the rural landscape as the proper setting for rustic views, they were stunned by the realities of the farming and industrializing countryside. Rural inhabitants of towns like Sutton, on the other hand, could not help but see their communities as the center places they had long been. The towns were the source of their livelihoods and were overlaid with intricate webs of daily commerce. Politically powerful, economically successful, they had no reason to view themselves or their neighborhoods nostalgically, as a quaint peasantry needing social superiors to keep them from destroying themselves through debt and profligacy. The way to respectability lay not in remaining content with their lot in life, but in improving their homes and farms in accordance with commonly understood standards of taste and economy.

Underlying the contemporary and later criticisms of the New England countryside's dwellings was an assumption of rural cultural backwardness. Once lodged, it is not easy to dispel and persists in modern work on architecture and culture. The assumption goes hand-in-hand with the idea that Americans failed in their post-Revolution quest for cultural expression. True, rural New Englanders failed to live up to reformers' standards, but they built to the standards of the architects and their architectural pattern books. There was nothing particularly rural about these houses, and therein lay the problem from the reformers' perspective. If the farmer were a distinctive and necessary component of the new republic, then surely, argued the rural reformers, their houses must be just as distinctive. If virtue resides in the yeomanry, then surely we can read that virtue in their residences. Unfortunately for the critics of New England's rural domiciles, the same plans, building materials and massing could be found in more urban areas.[8] The quest for cultural expression had not failed, but it had resulted in a rebuilding contrary to rural reformers' vision, a rebuilding subsequently unrecognized for what it was by succeeding generations critical of the classical ell houses.

Recorded Properties

Property No. 1

Built: c. 1811

Plan: center chimney, hall/parlor, double pile

Frame: five-sided ridge, vertically sawn common purlins, hewn principle rafters

Height: two stories

Ells: not integral, rear ell composed of two structural sections, end room is oldest and may have been moved to this location from elsewhere on the property

Ell Frame: 1. five-sided ridge, vertically sawn common rafters; 2. five-sided ridge, hewn principle rafter; vertically sawn common purlin

Outbuildings: none

Original owner/builder: Peter Sibley

Property No. 9

Built: 1794

Plan: center hall, double pile

Frame: unknown

Height: two stories

Ells: original, rear

Ell Frame: ridge, common rafter, common purlin

Outbuildings: barn; corn crib moved here from other site by current owner

Original owner/builder: Lazarus LeBaron

Property No. 15

Built: c. 1817

Plan: entry lobby, hall/parlor, single pile, rear chimney stacks

Frame: unknown

Height: two stories

Ells: integral, rear

Ell Frame: unknown

Outbuildings: none

Original owner/builder: unknown

Property No. 21

Built: by 1774

Plan: center chimney, hall/parlor, double pile

Frame: principle rafter with collars, principle purlin

Height: two stories

Ells: added but not extant

Ell Frame: unknown

Outbuildings: none, barn that stood across road is no longer extant

Original owner/builder: unknown

Property No. 23

Built: c. 1757

Plan: center chimney, hall/parlor, double pile

Frame: diamond ridge; principle rafter; principle purlin; heavy wind braces, collars removed; first floor—transverse summer; second floor—transverse summer

Height: two stories

Ells: added rear, 1830; side, 1840

Ell Frame: unknown

Outbuildings: small barn

Original owner/builder: Stephen Waters

Property No. 26

Built: c. 1767; 1801–6

Plan: c. 1806 house—entry lobby, hall/parlor, single pile, end chimneys; c. 1767 house— unknown plan, center chimney

Frame: c. 1806 house—diamond ridgepole, sawn principle rafters, hewn common purlins, two-story gunstock posts, transverse summer visible on second floor

Height: two stories

Ells: small rear ell on c. 1806 house, not integral; c. 1767 house served as side ell to new main block

Ell Frame: unknown

Outbuildings: barn, carriage shed

Original owner/builder: of c. 1806 house—Ebenezer Phelps or Enoch Stockwell

Property No. 29

Built: 1727; altered c. 1799

Plan: first phase—center chimney, hall/parlor, single pile; second phase—center chimney, hall/ parlor, double pile

Frame: principle rafters, common purlins, collars, wind braces (all hewn). West end—two-story gunstock posts, first floor longitudinal summer, second floor transverse summer. East end—first floor gunstock prick posts, transverse summer; second floor gunstock corner posts, transverse summer

Height: two stories

Ells: side, added 1806

Ell Frame: unknown

Outbuildings: barn, post-1860

Original owner/builder: Cornelius Putnam

Property No. 32

Built: c. 1810

Plan: center hall, double pile

Frame: five-sided ridge, principle rafters, common purlins

Height: two stories

Ells: original, made of older structure already on site

Ell Frame: unknown

Outbuildings: modern barn

Original owner/builder: probably Daniel Putnam

Property No. 36

Built: early nineteenth century

Plan: four-bay English barn

Frame: mortise and tenon, straight posts, roof replaced with nailed common rafters

Height: unknown

Ells: unknown

Ell Frame: unknown

Outbuildings: unknown

Original owner/builder: Benjamin Robinson

Property No. 43

Built: c. 1786(?)

Plan: gutted

Frame: common purlins

Height: two stories

Ells: unknown

Ell Frame: unknown

Outbuildings: barn cellar only

Original owner/builder: possibly Job Sibley

Property No. 47

Built: c. 1818–24

Plan: entry lobby, hall/parlor, double pile, interior chimneys

Frame: five-sided ridge, hewn common rafters

Height: two stories

Ells: side, integral, built as one story

Ell Frame: unknown

Outbuildings: barn, c. 1830–39; icehouse; shop

Original owner/builder: Joshua Armsby Jr.

Property No. 49

Built: 1825

Plan: entry lobby, hall/parlor, single pile, rear chimney stacks

Frame: main house—hip with five-sided ridge

Height: two stories

Ells: integral rear

Ell Frame: five-sided ridge, common rafters

Outbuildings: none

Original owner/builder: Avery Ward

Property No. 54

Built: c. 1765 in current form

Plan: center chimney, hall/parlor, double pile

Frame: five-sided ridge, common rafters

Height: two stories

Ells: gone

Ell Frame: unknown

Outbuildings: none

Original owner/builder: possibly Reuben Sibley

Property No. 55

Built: c. 1763

Plan: center hall, double pile

Frame: diamond ridge, principle rafters, common purlins, heavily braced, longitudinal summers

Height: one-and-a-half stories

Ells: rear, added by 1810; later side ell not extant

Ell Frame: unknown

Outbuildings: barn, two sheds

Original owner/builder: Malachi Marble

Property No. 57

Built: 1815

Plan: center hall, double pile

Frame: five-sided ridge, common rafters with purlin-like beam near floor supported by post and brace

Height: two stories

Ells: integral rear

Ell Frame: unknown

Outbuildings: attached barn, post-1850

Original owner/builder: Timothy Burnap

Property No. 58

Built: by 1732; enlarged by 1756

Plan: first phase—end chimney, single cell; second phase—center chimney, hall/parlor, single pile with rear lean-to

Frame: diamond ridge, principle rafters, common purlins, first floor summers longitudinal, second floor summers transverse

Height: two stories

Ells: added east end c. 1806; west end c. 1819?

Ell Frame: unknown

Outbuildings: none

Original owner/builder: Joseph Severy; Nathaniel Hutchinson

Property No. 61

Built: by 1734

Plan: main house and ell gutted

Frame: main house—principle rafter, common purlin gambrel roof with collars

Height: two stories

Ells: side, may have been original structure, serves as side ell now

Ell Frame: unknown

Outbuildings: none

Original owner/builder: Timothy Holton

Property No. 63

Built: 1835–38

Plan: entry lobby, hall/parlor, double pile, interior chimneys

Frame: five-sided ridge, common rafters with collars

Height: two stories

Ells: integral side ell

Ell Frame: unknown

Outbuildings: none

Original owner/builder: Zadok Woodbury

Property No. 69

Built: mid-eighteenth century(?)

Plan: first phase—probably center chimney, hall/parlor, single pile; second phase—center hall, double pile

Frame: principle rafters, common purlins, two-story gunstock posts

Height: two stories

Ells: side ell added

Ell Frame: unknown

Outbuildings: barn across street probably went to this property, now belongs to separate property

Original owner/builder: unknown

Property No. 70

Built: c. 1830

Plan: gutted

Frame: five-sided ridge, vertically sawn common rafters

Height: two stories

Ells: integral rear ell

Ell Frame: unknown

Outbuildings: none

Original owner/builder:
unknown

Property No. 80

Built: c. 1792

Plan: probably center chimney,
hall/parlor, single pile

Frame: five-sided ridge, collared
principle rafters (hewn)

Height: one story

Ells: gable end ell added in two stages,
early nineteenth century(?)

Ell Frame: first stage—hewn principle
rafters; second stage—vertically
sawn common rafters

Outbuildings: barn, two sheds

Original owner/builder: Benjamin
and Amos Batcheller

Property No. 82

Built: c. 1755–65

Plan: end chimney, single cell; altered
to center chimney, hall/parlor,
single pile

Frame: pegged common rafters,
first floor summers longitudinal,
second floor summers
transverse

Height: two stories

Ells: rear; added early nineteenth
century

Ell Frame: ridge board, common
rafters

Outbuildings: none

Original owner/builder: Dudley Chase;
Richard Hubbard Dodge

Property No. 91

Built: c. 1812

Plan: center chimney, hall/parlor,
double pile

Frame: five-sided ridge, vertically
sawn common rafters with single
purlin-like beam supported by
diagonal post and brace

Height: two stories

Ells: east end ell, not extant

Ell Frame: unknown

Outbuildings: none

Original owner/builder: Thomas
Harback(?)

Property No. 93

Built: c. 1750; c. 1780; c. 1800

Plan: end chimney, single cell;
altered to center chimney,
hall/parlor, single pile; altered
to center chimney, hall/parlor,
double pile

Frame: five-sided ridge, hewn principle
rafters, vertically sawn common
purlin, first floor summer beams
longitudinal, second floor
summers transverse

Height: two stories

Ells: rear ell c. 1810

Ell Frame: unknown

Outbuildings: none

Original owner/builder: John
Harback(?)

Property No. 94

Built: unknown

Plan: center chimney, hall/parlor,
double pile

Frame: principle rafters, common
purlins

Height: one story
Ells: rear ell
Ell Frame: gutted
Outbuildings: late-nineteenth-century barn
Original owner/builder: unknown

Property No. 95

Built: c. 1735–45; 1752; 1793
Plan: end chimney, single cell; altered to center chimney, hall/parlor, single pile; altered to center chimney, hall/parlor, double pile
Frame: east end—collared principle rafters, transverse summers both floors; west end—principle rafters, common purlins, first floor summer longitudinal
Height: two stories
Ells: side ell attached to house by breezeway, early nineteenth century
Ell Frame: unknown
Outbuildings: shed, barn
Original owner/builder: Stephen Hall

Property No. 101

Built: 1811–15
Plan: entry lobby, hall/parlor, single pile, rear chimney stacks
Frame: split planks used in place of studs
Height: two stories
Ells: integral rear ell extended in early nineteenth century
Ell Frame: extension—five-sided ridge, common rafters
Outbuildings: none
Original owner/builder: John Morse

Property No. 102

Built: 1813
Plan: center hall, single pile
Frame: five-sided ridge, common rafters
Height: two stories
Ells: integral rear ell
Ell Frame: five-sided ridge
Outbuildings: none
Original owner/builder: Salmon Burdon

Property No. 103

Built: probably 1759
Plan: center chimney, hall/parlor, double pile
Frame: pegged principle rafters
Height: two stories
Ells: rear ell added late eighteenth or early nineteenth century
Ell Frame: five-sided ridge, common rafters
Outbuildings: late nineteenth or early twentieth century
Original owner/builder: possibly Rev. David Hall

Property No. 104

Built: by 1788
Plan: end chimney, single cell
Frame: principle rafters, common purlins, one-story gunstock posts
Height: one story
Ells: none
Ell Frame: unknown
Outbuildings: none
Original owner/builder: unknown

Property Owners' Personal Data

Property No. 1

Name: Peter Sibley
Born: 1749, Uxbridge
Died: 1825, Sutton
Title/occupation: yeoman
Married: 1780, Mary Keith
    of Killingly, Conn.
Held public office: no
Religion: Baptist
Built or rebuilt: c. 1811

Property No. 1

Name: John Sibley
Born: 1789, Uxbridge
Died: 1823, Sutton
Title/occupation: yeoman
Married: 1812, Betsey (?)
Held public office: no
Religion: unknown
Built or rebuilt: c. 1811

Property No. 9

Name: Lazarus LeBaron
Born: Barbados, West Indies (?)
Died: 1828, Sutton

Title/occupation: merchant
Married: 1767, Susanna Johannot
    of Boston; 1777, Hannah Chase;
    1783, Mary Chase; 1802, Mary
    Woodbury (last three of Sutton)
Held public office: yes
Religion: Congregationalist
Built or rebuilt: 1792

Property No. 14

Name: Sumner Bastow
Born: 1777
Died: 1845, Oxford
Title/occupation: lawyer, clerk
Married: 1811, Tamar Waters
    of Sutton
Held public office: yes
Religion: possibly Congregationalist,
    although he married the daughter
    of a Baptist preacher
Built or rebuilt: 1817

Property No. 15

Name: Jonathan Dudley
Born: 1798, Sutton
Died: 1847, Sutton

Title/occupation: merchant
Married: Sarah Torrey
Held public office: no
Religion: Congregationalist
Built or rebuilt: 1826

Property No. 23

Name: John Waters
Born: 1764, Sutton
Died: 1848, Sutton
Title/occupation: yeoman
Married: 1790, Huldah Howard of Oxford; 1796, Hannah Putnam of Sutton; after 1818, Hitty Kidder of Millbury
Held public office: yes
Religion: Baptist
Built or rebuilt: 1830, 1840

Property No. 23

Name: Nathan Waters
Born: 1799, Sutton
Died: Sutton
Title/occupation: unknown
Married: 1832, Ulva A. Putnam of Oxford
Held public office: no
Religion: unknown
Built or rebuilt: 1830, 1840

Property No. 26

Name: Ebenezer Phelps
Born: 1755, Sutton
Died: unknown
Title/occupation: millwright, yeoman

Married: c. 1796, Polly Russell of Oxford
Held public office: no
Religion: unknown
Built or rebuilt: c. 1806

Property No. 26

Name: Enoch Stockwell
Born: 1771, Sutton
Died: 1836, Sutton
Title/occupation: gentleman
Married: 1795, Nancy Fecham
Held public office: yes
Religion: Congregationalist
Built or rebuilt: c. 1806

Property No. 29

Name: Nathaniel Putnam
Born: 1734, Putnam
Died: 1812, Sutton
Title/occupation: unknown
Married: 1756, Deborah Towne
Held public office: no
Religion: unknown
Built or rebuilt: 1806

Property No. 29

Name: Moses Putnam
Born: 1758, Sutton
Died: 1826, Sutton
Title/occupation: yeoman
Married: 1779, Mary Allen of Sutton
Held public office: no
Religion: unknown
Built or rebuilt: 1806

Property No. 47

Name: Joshua Armsby Jr.
Born: 1787, Foxborough
Died: 1858, Sutton
Title/occupation: housewright
Married: 1813, Martha McClellan;
    1823, Sara Woodbury (both
    of Sutton)
Held public office: yes
Religion: unknown
Built or rebuilt: c. 1824

Property No. 49

Name: Avery Ward
Born: 1794, Southborough
Died: 1879, Sutton
Title/occupation: yeoman
Married: 1814, Jane Maynard of
    Southborough
Held public office: no
Religion: unknown
Built or rebuilt: 1825

Property No. 55

Name: Malachi Marble
Born: 1736, Sutton
Died: 1811, Sutton
Title/occupation: husbandman
Married: 1761; 1786, Abigail Keyes
Held public office: yes
Religion: Congregationalist
Built or rebuilt: c. 1763, c. 1800

Property No. 57

Name: Timothy Burnap Jr.
Born: 1786, Sutton

Died: 1858, Sutton
Title/occupation: unknown
Married: 1815, Dolly Harback
Held public office: yes
Religion: Congregationalist
Built or rebuilt: 1815

Property No. 58

Name: Bartholomew Hutchinson
Born: 1734, Sutton
Died: 1820, Sutton
Title/occupation: gentleman
Married: 1763, Ruth Haven; c. 1797,
    Rebekah Monroe
Held public office: no
Religion: unknown
Built or rebuilt: c. 1806, c. 1819

Property No. 58

Name: Simon Hutchinson
Born: 1779, Sutton
Died: 1865, Sutton
Title/occupation: yeoman
Married: c. 1808, Vandalinda
    Morse; after 1830, Mrs. Sophia
    Batcheller (both of Sutton)
Held public office: yes
Religion: unknown
Built or rebuilt: c. 1806, c. 1819

Property No. 63

Name: Zadok Woodbury
Born: 1787, Sutton
Died: 1851, Sutton
Title/occupation: esquire

Married: 1812, Lucy Cummings
    of Sutton
Held public office: yes
Religion: unknown
Built or rebuilt: 1835

Property No. 80

Name: Amos Batcheller
Born: 1768, Sutton
Died: 1832, Sutton
Title/occupation: yeoman
Married: 1795, Abigail Hall
    of Sutton
Held public office: yes
Religion: Congregationalist
Built or rebuilt: c. 1801

Property No. 95

Name: William Hall
Born: 1783, Sutton
Died: 1860, Sutton
Title/occupation: millwright,
    housewright
Married: by 1810, Almy Greene
    of Rhode Island

Held public office: no
Religion: unknown
Built or rebuilt: c. 1811

Property No. 101

Name: John Morse
Born: 1787, Sutton
Died: unknown
Title/occupation: tanner
Married: 1805, Polly Hathaway
    of Sutton
Held public office: no
Religion: unknown
Built or rebuilt: 1811

Property No. 102

Name: Salmon Burdon
Born: 1779, Sutton
Died: 1865, Sutton
Title/occupation: yeoman
Married: 1799, Polly (Mary) Taylor
    of Sutton
Held public office: yes
Religion: unknown
Built or rebuilt: 1813

Deed and Probate Abstracts

The paired numbers indicate book and page in the Worcester County land records.

Property 1

1795: Joshua Sibley, blacksmith of Sutton, to Ebenezer Burnap, blacksmith of Ward (Auburn) 126/253

1796: Ebenezer Burnap Jr., black-smith of Sutton, to Peter Sibley, yeoman of Uxbridge 131/287

1811: Peter Sibley, yeoman of Sutton, to John Sibley III, yeoman of Sutton 234/238

1823: John Sibley III of Sutton, probate, series A 53491

1825: Stephen Blanchard of Millbury to John Stockwell Jr. of Millbury 246/574

1827: John Stockwell Jr., gentleman of Sutton, to Nathan Lombard, cabinetmaker of Sutton 259/531

1834: Nathan Lombard, yeoman of Sutton, to Nathan A. Lombard, machinist of Worcester 300/373

1839: Nathan Lombard, yeoman of Sutton, to Alonson A. Lombard, yeoman of Sutton 297/485

Property 9

1777: Nathaniel Sibley, gentleman of Sutton, to Lazarus LeBaron, gentleman of Sutton 86/233

1828: Lazarus LeBaron, probate, series A 36723

1837: Mary LeBaron, probate, series A 36724

Property 15

1817: Execution of Jonathan Davis against Amasa Braman 206/233

1826: Jabez Hull, trader of Millbury, to George C. Earle, esquire of Sutton 253/336

1826: George C. Earle, esquire of Sutton, to Jonathan Dudley, merchant of Sutton 259/319

1845: Paris Tourtellot of Sutton to Mary Waters of Sutton 401/395

Property 23

1761: Richard Waters, housewright of Sutton, to Stephen Waters, husbandman of Sutton 80/271

1800: Stephen Waters, yeoman of Sutton, to John Waters, yeoman of Sutton 143/9

1848: John Waters, probate 89/428

Property 25

1794: Noah Stockwell, yeoman of Sutton, to Stephen Holbrook, yeoman of Milford 127/495

1823: Mary Holbrook, widow, and heirs of Stephen Holbrook, to Simeon Stockwell II of Sutton 246/193–95

1823: Simeon Stockwell II, yeoman of Sutton, mortgaged to Mary Holbrook, single woman of Sutton 236/119

Property 26

1801: David Lilley, yeoman of Sutton, to Ebenezer Phelps, millwright of Sutton 144/409

1806: Ebenezer Phelps, yeoman of Thompson, Conn., to Enoch Stockwell, gentleman of Sutton 68/140

1836: Enoch Stockwell, probate, series A 56270 and 781/304

1839: Nancy Stockwell of Sutton and George F. Stockwell of Charlton to Lewis Stockwell, wheelwright of Sutton 345/215

1840: Lewis Stockwell, wheelwright of Sutton, to George F. Stockwell, yeoman of Charlton 347/478

Property 29

1723: John Hutchinson Sr., husbandman of Salem, to Cornelius Putnam, potter of Salem 29/437

1736: Joseph Severy, yeoman of Sutton, to Cornelius Putnam, yeoman of Sutton 9/258

1761: Cornelius Putnam, probate, series A 48293

1812: Nathaniel Putnam, probate, series A 48425

1817: Moses Putnam, yeoman of Sutton, to Sylvanus Putnam and John Putnam Jr., yeomen of Sutton 208/87

1824: John Putnam, yeoman of Sutton, to Sylvanus Putnam, yeoman of Sutton 240/340

Property 32

1799: Simon Fuller, yeoman of Sutton, to Caleb and Tyler Marsh, yeomen of Sutton 134/661

1803: Caleb and Tyler Marsh, yeomen of Sutton, to Tarrant King, mason of Sutton 177/254

1810: Tarrant King, yeoman of Sutton, to Daniel Putnam, house carpenter of Sutton 177/364

1812: Daniel Putnam, house carpenter of Sutton, to Perley Stockwell, gentleman of Sutton 189/199

1824: Erastus Bates, cordwainer of Sutton, to Solomon King, yeoman of Sutton 240/64

Property 47

1818: Joshua Armsby Sr., clerk of Sutton, to Joshua Armsby Jr., housewright of Sutton 245/197

1858: Joshua Armsby Jr., probate, series A 1886

Property 49

1825: Thomas Harback, yeoman of Sutton, to Avery Ward, yeoman of Sutton 244/315

Property 54

1733: Simon Dakin, husbandman of Sutton, to Samuel Daggett, husbandman of Sutton 4/546

1753: Samuel Daggett, husbandman of Sutton, to Nathaniel Sibley, husbandman of Sutton 37/439

1771: Samuel Daggett, husbandman of Sutton, to Reuben Sibley, husbandman of Sutton 65/393

1784: Nathaniel Sibley, gentleman of Sutton, to Reuben Sibley, gentleman of Sutton 111/312 and 111/313

1805: Reuben Sibley, gentleman of Sutton, to Nathaniel Sibley Jr., gentleman of Sutton 245/172

1836: Nathaniel Sibley Jr., gentleman of Sutton, to Sylvester Sibley, manufacturer of Sutton 318/263

Property 55

1763: Freegrace Marble, yeoman of Sutton, to Malachi Marble, husbandman of Sutton 65/12

1810: Malachi Marble, probate, series A 38606

1822: Ezra Marble, yeoman of Sutton, to Simeon Marble, merchant of New Haven, Conn. 227/633

1827: Simeon Marble, merchant of New Haven, Conn., to Oliver Leland, machine maker of Uxbridge 276/257

1858: Oliver Leland of Sutton to Reuben Leland of Sutton 592/275

Property 57

1829–30: various parties sell and quit claim all rights to the property of Timothy Burnap Sr. to Timothy Burnap Jr. 282/530, 282/532

Property 58

1732: Joseph Severy, weaver of Sutton, to Nathaniel Hutchinson, yeoman of Salem 5/412

1806: Bartholomew Hutchinson, gentleman of Sutton, to Simon Hutchinson, yeoman of Sutton 179/616

1853: Simon Hutchinson, yeoman of Sutton, to Edwin H. Hutchinson, yeoman of Sutton 505/537

Property 61

1727: Obadiah Walker, yeoman of Sutton, to Timothy Holton, glazier of Sutton 4/641

1734: Amos Goodale, husbandman of Sutton, to Timothy Holton, husbandman of Sutton 4/258

1734: James Smith, merchant of
Boston, to Timothy Holton,
husbandman of Sutton
5/259

1739: Timothy Holton, probate
1/435, 2/52, 2/97

1758: David Hall, shopkeeper of
Sutton, to Ezekial Cole,
shopkeeper of Sutton 41/410

1760: John Holton, yeoman of
Sutton, to Ezekial Cole 41/411

1760: John Holton, probate 6/509,
187/521

1799: Ezekial Cole, probate 29/271

Property 63

1835: Palmer Marble and Tyler
Putnam, yeomen of Sutton,
to Zadok Woodbury, esquire
of Charlton 308/4

1835: Simeon Woodbury, gentleman
of Sutton, to Zadok Woodbury,
esquire of Charlton 308/4

Property 80

1746: David Batcheller, cooper
of Grafton, to Abraham
Batcheller, cooper of
Westborough 22/219

1792: Abraham Batcheller, gentleman of Sutton, to Amos and
Benjamin Batcheller, yeomen
of Sutton 113/547

1792: same parties 113/546

1801: Benjamin Batcheller, gentleman
of Sutton, to Amos Batcheller,
yeoman of Sutton 158/42

1844: Abigail Batcheller and William
Hall, executors of estate of
Amos Batcheller, to Amos
B. Stockwell, husbandman
of Sutton 386/275

Property 82

1755: Samuel Chase, gentleman
of Sutton, to Dudley Chase,
yeoman of Sutton 36/314

1764: Dudley Chase, husbandman
of Sutton, to Richard Hubbard
Dodge, husbandman of Sutton
52/185

1815: Richard Hubbard Dodge,
probate, series A 17130

Property 95

1735: Percival Hall, husbandman
of Sutton, to Stephen Hall,
husbandman of Sutton 10/67

1738: Percival Hall, yeoman of
Sutton, to Stephen Hall,
husbandman of Sutton 13/294

1779: Stephen Hall Sr., gentleman
of Sutton, to Stephen Hall Jr.,
yeoman of Sutton 81/242

1807: Amasa Roberts, gentleman
of Sutton, to William Hall,
housewright of Sutton 168/184

1811: Stephen Hall Jr., yeoman
of Sutton, to William Hall,
millwright of [illeg.] Rhode
Island 178/371

1859: William Hall of Sutton, to
John Patch Stockwell of
Sutton 612/646

Property 101

1811: Nathaniel F. Morse, physician
of Sutton, to John Morse,
tanner of Sutton 195/484

1815: John Morse, tanner of
Sutton, to Daniel Day,
yeoman of Winchendon
195/78

1816: Christopher Nason, tanner
of Sutton, mortgaged to
Daniel Day, yeoman of
Winchendon 200/356

1823: Execution against Christopher
Nason, sold to Jacob Marsh,
esquire of Sutton 234/528

Property 102

1827: John Burdon, yeoman of
Sutton, to Salmon Burdon,
yeoman of Sutton
280/181

Property 103

1729–59: owned by David Hall Sr.
and David Hall Jr. (*History of
the Town of Sutton*, 37–39)

1759: David Hall Jr. to Thomas
Hancock 41/10

1785: John Hancock to Elizah
Putnam 103/176

1787: Execution against Elizah
Putnam by Nathaniel Fellows
104/52

1790: Nathaniel Fellows, merchant
of Boston, to Stephen
Munroe, physician of Sutton
115/275

1828: Jonas Sibley of Sutton to David
March of Sutton 261/528

Notes

Introduction

1. For dismissal of the significance of the era, see William D. Shipman, "The Federal Style: From About 1790–1825," in *Maine Forms of American Architecture,* ed. Deborah Thompson (Camden, Maine: Downeast Magazine, for Colby Museum of Art, 1976), 84; and Fiske Kimball, *Domestic Architecture of the American Colonies and of the Early Republic* (1922; rpt., New York: Dover Publications, 1966), 145. For significance of the era see Edward A. Chappell, "Housing a Nation: The Transformation of Living Standards in Early America," in *Of Consuming Interests: The Style of Life in the Eighteenth Century,* ed. Cary Carson et al. (Charlottesville: Univ. Press of Virginia, for the United States Capitol Historical Society, 1994). See also J. Ritchie Garrison, *Landscape and Material Life in Franklin County, Massachusetts, 1770–1860* (Knoxville: Univ. of Tennessee Press, 1991); Bernard Herman, *Architecture and Rural Life in Central Delaware, 1700–1900* (Knoxville: Univ. of Tennessee Press, 1987); and Joseph S. Wood, *The New England Village* (Baltimore: Johns Hopkins Univ. Press, 1997).

2. Abbott Lowell Cummings, *The Framed Houses of Massachusetts Bay, 1625–1725* (Cambridge: Harvard Univ. Press, Belknap Press, 1979), especially chap. 3; Michael Steinitz, "Landmark and Shelter: Domestic Architecture in the Cultural Landscape of the Central Uplands of Massachusetts in the Eighteenth Century" (Ph.D. diss., Clark Univ., 1988); Thomas Hubka, *Big House, Little House, Back House, Barn: The Connected Farm Buildings of New England* (Hanover, N.H.: Univ. of New England Press, 1984).

3. Cummings, *Framed Houses,* 23. Eighty-two of the 144 houses, or 57 percent, that he observed for that study grew from one-room plans to center-chimney, hall-parlor plans; see also Abbott Lowell Cummings, *Massachusetts and Its First Period Houses: A Statistical Survey with Summary Abstracts of Structural History*

and Transcriptions of Building Documents (rpt. from *Architecture in Colonial Massachusetts,* vol. 51 of Publications of the Colonial Society of Massachusetts, Boston, 1979), in which he notes that thirty-eight out of ninety-two first period structures he studied, or 41 percent, are known to have been built initially as "half-houses," or single-room structures with a chimney bay.

4. Hubka, *Big House, Little House,* 3.

5. Wood, *New England Village.*

6. On the picturesque and its association with neoclassicism in England see J. Morduant Crook, *The Dilemma of Style: Architectural Ideas from the Picturesque to the Post-Modern* (Chicago: Univ. of Chicago Press, 1987), chaps. 1 and 7. For a discussion of the mediation between art and nature in the eighteenth-century English countryside and the change in attitudes toward what was appropriately sited in a country setting see Diana Balmori, "Architecture, Landscape, and the Intermediate Structure: Eighteenth-Century Experiments in Mediation," *Journal of the Society of Architectural Historians* 50, no. 1 (Mar. 1991): 38–56. On the Georgianization of American vernacular building see Henry Glassie, *Folk Housing in Middle Virginia* (Knoxville: Univ. of Tennessee Press, 1975); Glassie, "Eighteenth-Century Cultural Process in Delaware Valley Folk Building," *Winterthur Portfolio* 7 (1972): 29–57; and James Deetz, *In Small Things Forgotten: The Archaeology of Early American Life* (New York: Anchor Books, 1977).

7. Cathy N. Davidson, *Revolution and the Word: The Rise of the Novel in America* (New York: Oxford Univ. Press, 1986), 13, and chaps. 3 and 4, especially pp. 49, 51, 79.

8. Richard L. Bushman, *The Refinement of America: Persons, Houses, Cities* (New York: Vintage Books, 1993).

9. Ibid., xvi.

10. Population grew between 6 and 12 percent each decade. Figures derived from population censuses reported in *History of Worcester County, Massachusetts* (Boston: C. F. Jewett, 1879), 27. Dwelling, barn, and shop numbers are reported in the Sutton data in the Worcester County Decennial Valuations, Worcester County, Mass., Papers, 1665–c. 1954, oversize vol. 2, ms., American Antiquarian Society, Worcester, Mass.

11. For a case study of the increasing efficiency of farms and industriousness of farmers see Robert Gross, "Culture and Cultivation: Agriculture and Society in Thoreau's Concord," in *Material Life in America,* ed. Robert St. George (Boston: Northeastern Univ., 1988), 519–33. Thomas Dublin defines out-work as "the distribution of raw materials to farm families for fabrication and

subsequent sale beyond the local market." See his "Women and Outwork in a Nineteenth-Century New England Town, Fitzwilliam, New Hampshire, 1830–1850," in *The Countryside in the Age of Capitalist Transformation: Essays in the Social History of Rural America,* ed. Steven Hahn and Jonathan Prude (Chapel Hill: Univ. of North Carolina Press, 1985), 52.

12. See Robert P. Swierenga, "Theoretical Perspectives on the New Rural History: From Environmentalism to Modernization," *Agricultural History* 56 (1982): 495–502; Thomas Bender, *Toward an Urban Vision: Ideas and Institutions in Nineteenth-Century America* (Baltimore: Johns Hopkins Univ. Press, 1975), wherein he argues that in the mid-nineteenth century a vision of urban culture existed that was an attempt to combine values traditionally associated with rural life with the perceived benefits of urban life; Richard D. Brown, "The Emergence of Urban Society in Rural Massachusetts, 1760–1820," *Journal of American History* 61 (June 1974): 29–51; and William Cronon, *Nature's Metropolis: Chicago and the Great West* (New York: W. W. Norton, 1991).

13. Glassie, *Folk Housing,* 111.

Chapter 1

1. Josiah Quincy, "An Address Delivered Before the Massachusetts Agricultural Society, at the Brighton Cattle Show, October 12, 1819," *Massachusetts Agricultural Repository and Journal* 6 (Jan. 1820): 10–11.

2. Ibid.

3. For discussion of the development of the romantic view of nature and farming see Paul H. Johnstone, "Turnips and Romanticism," *Agricultural History* 12 (July 1938): 224–55.

4. Anthony Low, *The Georgic Revolution* (Princeton: Princeton Univ. Press, 1985).

5. Richard Elsam, *Hints for Improving the Condition of the Peasantry in all Parts of the United Kingdom, by Promoting Comfort in their Habitation* (London: R. Ackerman, 1816), 14.

6. On the post-Revolution rebuilding of country estates around Boston see Charles Arthur Hammond, "'Where the Arts and the Virtues Unite': Country Life Near Boston, 1637–1864" (Ph.D. diss., Boston Univ., 1982), especially chaps. 2 and 3. Ann Bermingham discusses the eighteenth- and early-nineteenth-century English middle-class perception of the countryside as rustic landscape, and the relationship of that perception to the enclosure of rural England in her *Landscape and Ideology: The English Rustic Tradition, 1740–1860* (Berkeley: Univ. of California Press, 1986). See also Sarah Burns,

Pastoral Inventions: Rural Life in Nineteenth-Century American Art and Culture (Philadelphia: Temple Univ. Press, 1989).

7. Burns, *Pastoral Inventions,* 7, 17.

8. Brown, "Emergence of Urban Society," 29–51.

9. *Massachusetts Yeoman and Worcester Saturday Journal and Advertiser,* Oct. 25, 1825. Original emphasis.

10. For a discussion of the equation of enlightenment with classicism, and antiquity with republicanism see Gordon Wood, *The Radicalism of the American Revolution* (New York: Alfred A. Knopf, 1992), 100.

11. Jared Eliot, *Essays upon Field Husbandry in New England and Other Papers, 1748–1762,* ed. H. J. Carmen, R. G. Tugwell, R. H. True (New York: Columbia Univ. Press, 1934), 3. All references to Eliot's writings are from this edition.

12. Ibid., 97.

13. James Bannister, "On Architecture," *Massachusetts Magazine, or Monthly Museum of Knowledge and Rational Entertainment* (June 1789): 365.

14. Eliot, *Essays,* 34.

15. Paul H. Johnstone, "In Praise of Husbandry," *Agricultural History* 11 (Apr. 1937): 82.

16. Tamara Thornton, *Cultivating Gentlemen: The Meaning of Country Life among the Boston Elite: 1785–1860* (New Haven: Yale Univ. Press, 1989).

17. Alan Taylor, *Liberty Men and Great Proprietors: The Revolutionary Settlement on the Maine Frontier, 1760–1820* (Chapel Hill: Univ. of North Carolina Press for the Institute of Early American History and Culture, 1990). See also Laurel Thatcher Ulrich, *A Midwife's Tale: The Life of Martha Ballard, Based on Her Diary 1785–1812* (New York: Alfred A. Knopf, 1990), 319–35, for the effect of the Malta uprising in the territory of Maine on one family.

18. Nathan Fiske, *The Moral Monitor,* 2 vols. (Worcester, Mass.: Isaiah Thomas Jr., 1801). Thomas initially published the essays in the *Massachusetts Spy* and the *Massachusetts Magazine* in Worcester. Thomas himself was a member of both the MSPA and the Worcester Agriculture Society.

19. Ibid., 1: 139.

20. Ibid., 2: 288.

21. Ibid., 2: 164.

22. Ibid.

23. Ibid., 2: 105–6.

24. John Brooke, *The Heart of the Commonwealth: Society and Political Culture in Worcester County, Massachusetts, 1713–1861* (Cambridge: Cambridge Univ. Press, 1989), 249–68.

25. David Humphreys, *A Discourse on the Agriculture of the State of Connecticut, and the Means of Making it more Beneficial to the State. Delivered to the Society for Promoting Agriculture in Connecticut, New Haven, Sept. 12, 1816.* (New Haven: T. G. Woodward, 1816), 8, 24.

26. Lewis Bigelow, *Address Delivered Before the Worcester Agricultural Society, October 12, 1820* (Worcester, Mass.: Manning and Trumbell, 1821), 3. Bigelow joined the Worcester Agriculture Society in 1819, but was not a member of the MSPA. For information on Bigelow see Charles Nutt, *History of Worcester and Its People* (New York: Lewis Historical Publishing, 1919), 3: 401. For membership of the Worcester Agriculture Society see *Catalogue of Members of the Worcester Agriculture Society* (Worcester, Mass.: Moses W. Grout, 1832). For MSPA members see Hammond, "Where the Arts and Virtue Unite," Appendix A; and amendments to that list by Andrew Baker, Old Sturbridge Village, Research Department files, Sturbridge, Mass.

27. *New England Farmer* 3 (Dec. 10, 1824): 153–55.

28. Biographical material on Goodwin from American Antiquarian Society ms. holding summary.

29. Henry Coleman, *An Address before the Hampshire, Franklin and Hampden Agricultural Society, delivered in Greenfield, Oct. 23, 1833* (Greenfield, Mass.: Phelps and Ingersoll, 1833), 24.

30. Enos Hitchcock, *The Farmer's Friend: or the History of Mr. Charles Worthy* (Boston: Isaiah Thomas and E. T. Andrews, 1793).

31. For a discussion of the eighteenth-century origins of the popularization of the link between taste and virtue and the subsequent imbuing of taste with spirituality see Colin Campbell, *The Romantic Ethic and the Spirit of Modern Consumerism* (Oxford: Basil Blackwell, 1987), 150–59, 182. For the integration of new, picturesque theories of landscape design into country estates around Boston, see Hammond, "'Where the Arts and Virtue Unite,'" 73–135.

32. "Review of Essays on the Nature and Principles of Taste," *General Repository and Review,* Jan. 1813, 212–13.

33. Timothy Dwight, *Travels in New England and New York,* 4 vols., ed. Barbara M. Solomon (1822; rpt., Cambridge: Harvard Univ. Press, Belknap Press, 1969), 1: 269.

34. Ibid.

35. Ibid., 1: 132.

36. Ibid., 2: 179.

37. Ibid., 1: 154.

38. Richard Bushman, "A Poet, A Planter, and a Nation of Farmers," *Journal of Early America* 19 (Spring 1999): 1–14.

39. Samuel Denny, *The Farmer: A Practical Treatise on Agriculture* (Brookfield: E. and G. Merriam, 1824), 24.

40. *New England Farmer* 8, no. 12 (Oct. 9, 1829): 94.

41. *New England Farmer* 1, no. 45 (June 7, 1823): 353.

42. Rpt. in the *Massachusetts Yeoman and Worcester Saturday Journal and Advertiser* 3, no. 43 (June 17, 1826): 172.

43. Campbell, *Romantic Ethic,* 150–54.

44. William Dunlap, *History of the Rise and Progress of the Arts of Design in the United States,* 2 vols. (New York: George P. Scott, 1834), 1: 335. For a discussion of the moral implications of domestic design in the late nineteenth and early twentieth centuries see Gwendolyn Wright, *Moralism and the Model Home: Domestic Architecture and Cultural Conflict in Chicago* (Chicago: Univ. of Chicago Press, 1980).

45. A. J. Downing, *Rural Essays,* ed. George William Curtis (New York: George P. Putnam, 1853), 230.

46. William Ranlett, *The Architect: A Series of Original Designs, for Domestic and Ornamental Cottages and Villas,* 2 vols. (vol. 1, New York: William H. Graham, 1847; vol. 2, New York: Dewitt and Davenport, 1849), 1: 3.

47. Daniel Vickers, "Competence and Competition: Economic Culture in Early America," *William and Mary Quarterly* 47, no. 1 (1990): 7.

48. Bushman, "Poet, a Planter, and a Nation of Farmers," 1–14.

49. Rpt. from the *Taunton Advocate* in the *New England Farmer* 7, no. 25 (Jan. 9, 1829): 195.

50. Rpt. from the *Genesee Farmer* in the *New England Farmer* 10, no. 36 (Mar. 21, 1832): 288.

51. Minard Lafever, *The Young Builder's General Instructor* (Newark: W. Tuttle, 1829), 157.

52. *New England Farmer* 1, no. 45 (June 7, 1823): 353.

53. *New England Farmer* 4, no. 6 (Sept. 2, 1825): 45.

54. On the interest of gentlemen farmers and the MSPA in horticulture see Thornton, *Cultivating Gentlemen*; and Hammond, "'Where the Arts and Virtue Unite,'" especially 132–38 and 160–63.

55. See Bermingham, *Landscape and Ideology.*

56. Rpt. from the *National Aegis* in the *New England Farmer* 8, no. 1 (July 25, 1828): 5.

57. *New England Farmer* 11, no. 28 (Jan. 23, 1833): 218.

58. Winifred Rothenberg, *From Market-Places to a Market Economy: The Transformation of Rural Massachusetts, 1750–1850* (Chicago: Univ. of Chicago Press, 1992), 120–21.

59. See Appendices A and B, property nos. 1, 9, 14, 15, 23, 26, 29, 47, 49, 55, 57, 58, 63, 80, 95, 101, and 102. Property no. 14 was observed only from the road. The others were all recorded in detail during site visits. These properties represent all of those surveyed for which construction or rebuilding dates are known.

60. Derived from the twenty individuals for whom birthdate and exact or approximate improvement dates were known. The improvements consisted of either adding an ell to an older house or building a new house.

61. Sutton schedules, 1798 Direct Tax Census. Eliminating the highest ($2,000) and lowest ($103) home lot values, the average for the group becomes $485, still half again as much as the town-wide average.

62. Based on the nine properties still owned by those who had made improvements, or were about to make improvements. Sutton Town Tax Valuation, 1830.

63. This will result in an undercount as mothers' families are not taken into account, nor are the families into which siblings and children married. In addition, families bearing the names of the study group who moved out of Sutton and into surrounding communities are not counted. They, too, would have been close enough to participate in kin networks.

64. Family names of husbands and wives were counted in the 1798 Direct Tax Census, and the 1830 Sutton Town Tax Valuation. The average number of related households per individual was 10.6 in 1798, 9.7 in 1830. On the importance of kinship networks see Garrison, *Landscape and Material Life,* 33–41.

65. *Vital Records of Sutton, Massachusetts, To the End of the Year 1849* (Worcester, Mass.: Franklin P. Rice, for the Systematic History Fund, 1907).

66. Worcester County Probate Court, Worcester County Courthouse, Nathaniel Putnam will, series A, case 48425. This property, although not devised exactly as Nathaniel wished, remained in the Putnam family at the close of the twentieth century.

67. Taylor, *Liberty Men and Great Proprietors,* 61–87.

68. Households counted from Federal Decennial Censuses of 1800 and 1830. Number of dwellings taken from 1800 Decennial Census and Worcester County Valuation Record Book, 1801–1831, Worcester County, Mass., papers, ms., American Antiquarian Society, Worcester, Mass.

69. This description is based on a circa 1878 wood engraving in William A. Benedict and Hiram A. Tracy, *History of the Town of Sutton, 1704–1876* (1878; 2nd rpt., 1970), 232.

70. Worcester County Probate, Worcester County Courthouse, Enoch Stockwell, series A, case 56270.

71. These related households usually consisted of parents and one married offspring with his or her family. I found no instances of married siblings cohabiting. On similar household composition in the seventeenth century see John Demos, *A Little Commonwealth: Family Life in Plymouth Colony* (London: Oxford Univ. Press, 1970), 62–64, 75–81.

72. Quoted in Harriet M. Forbes, "Elias Carter, Architect, of Worcester, Massachusetts," *Old Time New England* 11 (1920): 68.

73. J. G. A. Pocock, "Virtue and Commerce in the Eighteenth Century," *Journal of Interdisciplinary History* 3 (1972): 124–25, 129.

74. Ibid., 133.

Chapter 2

1. "On the Progress of the Arts," *Massachusetts Magazine* 1 (Apr. 1789): 240.

2. Hugh Honour, *Neoclassicism* (New York: Penguin Books, 1977), 14; John Summerson, *Architecture in Britain, 1530–1830* (New York: Penguin Books, 1977), 409; Robert Morris, *Select Architecture,* 2nd ed. (London: Robert Sayer, 1757), introduction, n.p.

3. Bannister, "On Architecture," 401.

4. As quoted in Joseph J. Ellis, *After the Revolution: Profiles of Early American Culture* (New York: W. W. Norton, 1979), 4.

5. Antoinette F. Downing and Vincent J. Scully Jr., *The Architectural Heritage of Newport, Rhode Island, 1640–1915,* 2nd rev. ed. (New York: American Legacy

Press, 1967), 46, 84–86; Carl Bridenbaugh, *Peter Harrison: The First American Architect* (Chapel Hill: Univ. of North Carolina Press, for the Institute of Early American History and Culture, 1949), 103.

6. Richard Elsam, *An Essay on Rural Architecture* (London: St. George's Fields Philanthropic Society, 1803), 1–6.

7. On neoclassicism as a pejorative term see Honour, *Neoclassicism,* 14.

8. For an analysis of the rebuilding on a national scale see Chappell, "Housing a Nation"; Frank Cousins, and Phil M. Riley, *The Colonial Architecture of Salem* (Boston: Little, Brown, 1919); Kimball, *Domestic Architecture*; Garrison, *Landscape and Material Life*; and Herman, *Architecture and Rural Life.* The last two both offer in-depth analyses of their respective study areas for this time period.

9. "The New Stone Church," *Boston Spectator* 1 (Dec. 31, 1814): 210.

10. On neoclassicism as an international movement see Honour, *Neoclassicism.*

11. On classicism, morality and the perfectibility of society see L. E. A. Eitner, *Neoclassicism and Romanticism, 1750–1850* (Englewood Cliffs, N. J.: Prentice Hall, 1970); Honour, *Neoclassicism.*

12. On the spread of classicism see Neil Harris, "The Making of an American Culture: 1750–1800," and Jules David Prown, "Style in American Art, 1750–1800," both in *American Art, 1750–1800: Towards Independence,* ed. Charles Montgomery and Patricia Kane (Boston: New York Graphic Society, 1976).

13. Bulfinch employed the lower roof pitch by 1795. See Harold Kirker and James Kirker, *Bulfinch's Boston, 1787–1817* (New York: Oxford Univ. Press, 1964). McIntire employed a balustrade at the eave as early as 1782, but continued to design houses with high-hipped roofs in the 1790s. See Fiske Kimball, *Mr. Samuel McIntire, Carver, the Architect of Salem* (Portland, Maine: Southworth-Anthoensen Press, 1940), 34.

14. Kirker and Kirker point out that Bulfinch "never entirely shook off colonial or Palladian traditions." They attribute this primarily to Boston's aesthetic provincialism, rather than to Bulfinch's own inclinations (*Bulfinch's Boston,* 31–32).

15. Ibid., 51.

16. On the influence of eighteenth-century English architectural books see Kimball, *Domestic Architecture,* 55–63.

17. Owen Biddle, *An Improved and Enlarged Edition of Biddle's Carpenter's Assistant,* ed. John Haviland (Philadelphia: M. Polock, 1858), from the preface to the first edition, 4.

18. Dell Upton, "Pattern Books and Professionalism: Aspects of the Transformation of Domestic Architecture in America, 1800–1860," *Winterthur Portfolio* 19 (Summer–Autumn 1984): 115.

19. Asher Benjamin and Daniel Raynard, *The American Builder's Companion: or a New System of Architecture, Particularly Adapted to the Present Style of the United States of America* (Boston: Etheridge and Bliss, 1806), viii.

20. On Asher Benjamin and American distinctiveness see Jack Quinan, "Asher Benjamin and American Architecture," *Journal of the Society of Architectural Historians* 38 (Oct. 1979): 241–61.

21. Upton, "Pattern Books," 15.

22. On the role of the middle class in creating taste see Honour, *Neoclassicism,* 87; on middle-class consumption and taste see Campbell, *Romantic Ethic.*

23. Brown, "Emergence of Urban Society," 29–51.

24. James Henretta et al., *America's History: Vol. 1 to 1877* (New York: Worth Publishers, 1997), A-10.

25. David Hackett Fischer, *Paul Revere's Ride* (New York: Oxford Univ. Press, 1994), 300.

26. *Historic Events of Worcester: A Brief Account* (Boston: Walton Advertising and Printing, 1922), 8–11.

27. See Richard D. Brown, *The Strength of a People: The Idea of an Informed Citizenry in America, 1650–1870* (Chapel Hill: Univ. of North Carolina Press, 1996), 53, for a discussion of Boston's Whigs and the broadening of the franchise.

28. Stanley Elkins and Erik McKitrick, *The Age of Federalism* (New York: Oxford Univ. Press, 1993), 168–69.

29. David Jaffee, *People of the Wachusett: Greater New England in History and Memory, 1630–1860* (Ithaca: Cornell Univ. Press, 1999), especially chap. 6.

30. Ibid., 219.

31. "Architecture in the United States," *American Journal of Science and Arts* 17 (Jan. 1830): 99, 108; and "Architecture in the United States," part 4, *American Journal of Science and Arts* (June 1830): 232.

32. Elkins and McKitrick, 163.

33. See Richard Bushman, "American High-Style and Vernacular Cultures," in *Colonial British America: Essays in the New History of the Early Modern Era,* ed. Jack P. Greene and J. R. Pole (Baltimore: Johns Hopkins Univ. Press, 1984), 345–83.

34. Bushman, "American High-Style," 353.

35. Alan Taylor, *William Cooper's Town: Power and Persuasion on the Frontier of the Early American Republic* (New York: Vintage Books, 1996).

36. Bushman, "American High-Style," 365.

37. Dell Upton, "White and Black Landscapes in Eighteenth-Century Virginia," in *Material Life in America, 1600–1860,* ed. Robert B. St. George (Boston: Northeastern Univ. Press), 357–69; Campbell, *Romantic Ethic,* 159–63.

38. Bushman, "American High-Style," 365.

39. On the inadequacy of social emulation theory see Campbell, *Romantic Ethic,* 24–33.

40. Brooke, *Heart of the Commonwealth.*

41. Henry Cleveland, "American Architecture," *North American Review* 43 (Oct. 1836): 382.

42. George Tucker, "Thoughts of a Hermit—For the Port Folio: On Architecture," *Port Folio* 4 (1814): 559–69.

43. Cleveland, "American Architecture," 356.

44. Horatio Greenough, *The Travels, Observations, and Experience of a Yankee Stonecutter* (New York, 1852), excerpted and rpt. in *America Builds: Source Documents in American Architecture and Planning,* ed. Leland Roth (New York: Harper and Row, 1983), 78, 81.

45. Ranlett, *Architect,* 1: 38, 2: 39 for first two assertions; Downing, *Rural Essays,* 248.

46. Downing, *Rural Essays,* 389.

47. Lewis F. Allen, *Rural Architecture* (New York: C. M. Saxton, 1853), xiii.

48. N. H. Chamberlain, *A Paper Read Before the New England Historic and Genealogical Society* (Boston: Crosby, Nichols, 1858), 10–12.

Chapter 3

1. Data from Brookfield, Mendon and Uxbridge gathered by Michael Steinitz and discussed in his "Rethinking Geographical Approaches to the Common House: The Evidence from Eighteenth-Century Massachusetts," in *Perspectives in Vernacular Architecture,* 3, ed. Thomas Carter and Bernard L. Herman (Columbia: Univ. of Missouri Press, 1989), 16–26. On agricultural surpluses, see Bettye Hobbs Pruitt, "Self-Sufficiency and the Agricultural Economy of Eighteenth-Century Massachusetts," *William and Mary Quarterly* 61 (July

1984): 333–64. On the mid-eighteenth-century rebuilding in western Massachusetts see Kevin Sweeney, "Mansion People: Kinship, Class, and Architecture in Western Massachusetts in the Mid-Eighteenth Century," *Winterthur Portfolio* 19 (Winter 1984): 231–55; and Garrison, *Landscape and Material Life,* 154–56. Of roughly forty extant eighteenth-century houses in Sutton, about twenty are two-story structures. Field work conducted by author.

2. Steinitz, "Rethinking," 20–21.

3. Cummings, *Framed Houses,* 16–17.

4. Ibid., 23.

5. See Appendix A, nos. 29, 58, 82, 93, 95.

6. Richard Candee, "'An Old Town By the Sea': Urban Landscapes and Vernacular Building in Portsmouth, New Hampshire, 1660–1990," Field Guide for Vernacular Architecture Forum Conference, 1992, Portsmouth, N.H., 9.

7. See Benedict and Tracy, *History of the Town of Sutton, 1704–1876,* 372 for the old dating; see Appendix A, no. 95.

8. Appendix A, no. 82.

9. Ibid., no. 104.

10. Ibid., no. 26.

11. Ibid., no. 23.

12. Lafever, *Young Builder's General Instructor,* 157.

13. Kimball dated the Foster-Hutchinson House to 1686, but Abbott Lowell Cummings has dated it to 1689–92. See his "The Foster-Hutchinson House," *Old Time New England* 54, no. 3 (Jan.–Mar. 1964), ser. no. 195: 58–76.

14. J. Frederick Kelly, *Early Domestic Architecture of Connecticut* (1924; rpt., New York: Dover Publications, 1963), 16–20; Kimball, *Domestic Architecture,* 44–46, 62, 70. For early examples in Rhode Island see Downing and Scully, *Architectural Heritage,* including Whitehall, 1729, pl. 85, and the Jonathan Nichols house, c. 1748, pl. 88–91.

15. Sweeney, "Mansion People," 238; Garrison, *Landscape and Material Life,* chap. 7.

16. Glassie, "Eighteenth-Century Cultural Process," 29–57; Deetz, *In Small Things Forgotten*; Dell Upton, "Vernacular Domestic Architecture in Eighteenth-Century Virginia," *Winterthur Portfolio* 17 (Summer–Autumn 1982): 95–119; Sweeney, "Mansion People," 231–55.

17. Kevin Sweeney, "High-Style Vernacular: Lifestyles of the Colonial Elite," in *Of Consuming Interests: The Style of Life in the Eighteenth Century,* ed. Cary

Carson, Ronald Hoffman, and Peter Albert (Charlottesville: Univ. Press of Virginia, for the United States Capitol Historical Society, 1994) discusses spatial arrangements as being conducive to the unity of peers rather than as promoting separation from inferiors; Mark Wenger, "Architecture and Privacy in Early Virginia" (paper delivered at Vernacular Architecture Forum Conference, May, 1998, Annapolis, Md.), discusses the impact of the increased importance of domesticity on spatial arrangements.

18. On the use of central-hall plans by the Connecticut River Valley River Gods, and its relative rarity throughout rural New England in the eighteenth century see Sweeney, "Mansion People," 238–39.

19. Worcester County Probate, Worcester County Courthouse, Worcester, Mass., series A, case 38606.

20. Lafever, *Young Builder's General Instructor,* 157.

21. Of the fourteen houses that I investigated in Sutton that were built between 1790 and 1840, three used older structures for ells, connecting them to the new house at the time of construction (see Appendix A, nos. 1, 26, 32); ten were built with integral ells or had them added shortly after construction (Appendix A, nos. 9, 15, 47, 49, 57, 63, 70, 80, 101, 102); and the last one had an ell, but it was removed prior to my investigation (Appendix A, no. 91). Twelve out of fourteen pre-1790 houses had ells added to them prior to 1850. Garrison, *Landscape and Material Life,* 163; Marla Miller, "Labor and Liberty in the Age of Refinement: Gender, Class and the Built Environment," paper delivered at the Vernacular Architecture Forum Conference, Duluth, Minn., June 2000; "'Old Town by the Sea,'" 10–11.

22. John Worlidge, "Explanation of the Frontispiece," *Systema Agriculturae: Being the Mystery of Husbandry Discovered and Layd Open,* 2nd ed. (1675; facsimile, Los Angeles: Sherwin and Freitel, 1970), n.p.

23. Morris, *Select Architecture,* introduction, n.p.

24. John Martin Robinson, *Georgian Model Farms: A Study of Decorative and Model Farm Buildings in the Age of Improvement, 1700–1846* (Oxford: Clarendon Press, 1983), 4.

25. Hitchcock, *Farmer's Friend,* 49.

26. Benjamin and Raynard, *American Builder's Companion,* 67.

27. Stephen William Johnson, *Rural Economy* (New Brunswick, N.Y.: William Elliot, for I. Riley and Co., 1806), 92.

28. Mrs. L. C. Tuthill, *History of Architecture* (1848; rpt., New York: Garland Publishing, 1988).

29. Mrs. H. M. Pierce Gallagher, *Robert Mills, Architect of the Washington Monument, 1781–1855* (1935; rpt., New York: AMS Press, 1966), 170.

30. Ruth H. Bloch, "The Gendered Meanings of Virtue in Revolutionary America," *Signs* 13, no. 1 (Autumn 1987): 37–58.

31. Hannah Barnard, *Dialogues on Domestic and Rural Economy*, 1820, dated pamphlets, American Antiquarian Society, Worcester, Mass., 13.

32. Worcester County Probate, Worcester County Courthouse, Nathaniel Putnam Estate, series A, case 48425.

33. Thomas Hubka found that the "little house" contained a kitchen while the "back house" contained workrooms such as dairy or laundry, storage space, and privy (*Big House, Little House*, 44–52).

Chapter 4

1. Benedict and Tracy, *History of the Town of Sutton*, 283.

2. John Stilgoe has touched on the phenomenon in *Metropolitan Corridor: Railroads and the American Scene* (New Haven: Yale Univ. Press, 1983), 329–33; James M. Lindgren deals with the subject in detail in *Preserving Historic New England: Preservation, Progressivism, and the Remaking of Memory* (New York: Oxford Univ. Press, 1995).

3. Joseph Wood's extensive work on the post-Revolution transformation of the New England townscape has been conveniently assembled in his *The New England Village*.

4. Gary Kulik, "Dams, Fish, and Farmers: Defense of Public Rights in Eighteenth-Century Rhode Island," in *The Countryside in the Age of Capitalist Transformation*, ed. Stephen Hahn and Jonathan Prude (Chapel Hill: Univ. of North Carolina Press, 1985); Thomas Dublin, "Women and Outwork in a Nineteenth-Century New England Town: Fitzwilliam, New Hampshire, 1830–1850," in *The Countryside in the Age of Capitalist Transformation*, ed. Hahn and Prude; Jonathan Prude, *The Coming of Industrial Order: Town and Factory Life in Rural Massachusetts, 1810–1860* (Cambridge: Cambridge Univ. Press, 1985).

5. Eliot, *Essays*, 7.

6. Ibid., 232.

7. *American Husbandry: Containing an Account of the Soil, Climate, Production, and Agriculture of the British Colonies*, ed. H. J. Carman and R. G. Tugwell (1775; rpt., New York: Columbia Univ. Press, 1939).

8. *American Husbandry,* 46. For myths of plenty in the New World see William Cronon, *Changes in the Land: Indians, Colonists, and the Ecology of New England* (New York: Hill and Wang, 1983), chap. 2. For the tradition of the American pastoral see Leo Marx, *The Machine in the Garden: Technology and the Pastoral Ideal in America* (New York: Oxford Univ. Press, 1984).

9. *American Husbandry,* 55.

10. Ibid., 55, 59.

11. Marquis de Chastellux, *Travels in North America in the years 1780–81–82* (New York, 1828), 31, 306.

12. Eliot, *Essays,* 83.

13. Dwight, *Travel,* 1: 272.

14. Archaeological evidence bears out the use of post fencing in Worcester County in the eighteenth and nineteenth centuries. See, for example, field reports of the Bixby site in Barre, Mass., and of the Freeman site in Sturbridge, Mass., at the Old Sturbridge Village Research Department, Sturbridge, Mass.

15. Worcester County Land Records, Worcester County Courthouse, Worcester, Mass., deed book 1, p. 55.

16. Worcester County Land Records, Worcester County Courthouse, deed book 5, p. 412; deed book 65, p. 12.

17. The qualifier "as the wall now stands" remained in use in some cases. The change in language of property boundaries was observed in 141 Sutton deeds dating from the 1720s to the 1860s, and in several partitions of land for widows' dowers from 1800 to 1850.

18. Among these are the *Ezekiel Hersey Derby Farm* (Salem, Mass.), by Michele Felice Corne, c. 1790; the *Farmhouse in Charlton, MA,* anonymous, early nineteenth century (collection of Mr. and Mrs. Barnes Riznik); *Ralph Wheelock's Farm* (Southbridge, Mass.), by Francis Alexander, c. 1822 (National Gallery of Art, Washington, D.C.).

19. See Hubka, *Big House, Little House,* 55.

20. Henry David Thoreau, *Walden* (New York: Holt, Rinehart and Winston, 1964), 46.

21. Henry Glassie, "The Variation of Concepts within Tradition: Barn Building in Otsego County, New York," in *Man and Cultural Heritage: Papers in Honor of Fred B. Kniffen,* ed. H. J. Walker and W. G. Haag, off-set print from *Geoscience and Man* 5 (June 1974): 182; Henry Glassie, "Barns across Southern England: A Note on Transatlantic Comparison and Architectural Meanings,"

Pioneer America 7 (1975): 9–19; Robert St. George, "The Stanley-Lake Barn in Topsfield, Massachusetts: Some Comments on Agricultural Buildings in Early New England," in *Perspectives in Vernacular Architecture* 1, ed. Camille Wells (Annapolis: Vernacular Architecture Forum, 1982), 7–23.

22. Robert St. George, "'Set Thine House in Order': The Domestication of the Yeomanry in Seventeenth-Century New England," in *New England Begins: The Seventeenth Century,* vol. 2, ed. J. L. Fairbanks and R. F. Trent (Boston: Museum of Fine Arts, 1982), 162.

23. Quote is from Samuel Symonds, letter to John Winthrop the younger, 1638, in Deetz, *In Small Things Forgotten,* 101. Deetz also discusses the archaeological evidence for longhouses but does not provide information on possible combinations of human and livestock habitation (96–97).

24. St. George, "'Set Thine House in Order,'" 165.

25. J. Ritchie Garrison analyzed outbuildings recorded in the 1798 Direct Tax lists for South Hadley and Colrain, Massachusetts as well as surviving farm structures from the mid-eighteenth to the early nineteenth century. See his "Rebuilding the Barn: Landscape, Barns and Outbuildings in Franklin County, MA, 1770–1870," paper delivered at Historic Deerfield Colloquium, Apr. 1991, specifically pp. 6–8.

26. Dr. Samuel Deane, *New England Farmer: or Georgical Dictionary,* 3rd ed. (Boston: Wells and Lilley, 1822), 16.

27. Dwight, *Travels,* 1: 272.

28. See also Garrison, "Rebuilding the Barn"; Glassie, "Variation of Concepts," 182.

29. *New England Farmer* 3, no. 11 (Oct. 9, 1824): 81–82.

30. Appendix A, property no. 36. Robinson's house dated in Benedict and Tracy, *History of the Town of Sutton,* 343.

31. *Massachusetts Yeoman* 3 (Nov. 26, 1825): 1.

32. Garrison, "Rebuilding the Barn," 14.

33. See, for example, *New England Farmer* (ed. Thomas Fessenden) 1, no. 45 (June 7, 1823): 353; and Thomas Fessenden, *The Complete Farmer and Rural Economist* (Boston: Lilley, Wait and Co. and George C. Barrett, New England Farmer Office, 1834), 73.

34. It was raised to two stories early in the twentieth century.

35. *New England Farmer* 1, no. 45 (June 7, 1823): 353.

36. Sutton Town Tax Valuation Lists, 1830, Sutton Town Hall.

37. In 1830 the average taxed land parcel size was 58.4 acres.

38. Stephen Holbrook Probate Inventory, book 53: 252; Worcester County Land Records, 246: 193–95; 236: 119; Benedict and Tracy, *History of Sutton,* 234.

39. Worcester County Probate Records, Worcester County Courthouse, Enoch Stockwell estate, series A, case 56270.

40. Construction date of this barn is extrapolated from Sutton tax valuations of 1830 and 1835 for John Woodbury and his son Nathaniel Woodbury. Size and framing information is from an unpublished survey of Worcester County barns conducted by John Mott and Frank White for Old Sturbridge Village from 1976 to 1978. The survey is located in the Research Dept. of Old Sturbridge Village, Sturbridge, Mass.; John Woodbury died 1831; see Benedict and Tracy, *History of Sutton,* 751.

41. Changes determined from the Sutton data in the Worcester County Decennial Valuation, Worcester County, Mass., papers, 1665–c. 1954, oversize vol. 2, ms., American Antiquarian Society, Worcester, Mass.

42. This discussion relies on the information gathered by Mott and White (Old Sturbridge Village) in the mid-1970s. Many of the barns they surveyed are gone.

43. Although cellars were by far more numerous in the later New England barns than in the English barns, cellars were not an inevitable part of New England barns. In other parts of the country in the early nineteenth century, English-type barns, with entrances on their long sides, were regularly built with cellars, while gable-entrance barns were commonly built without. See Glassie, "Variation of Concepts," 185–90, for examples in upstate New York; and Glassie, *Pattern in the Material Folk Culture of the Eastern United States* (Philadelphia: Univ. of Pennsylvania Press, 1968), 60–61, for examples in Pennsylvania.

44. Domestic economy and rural economy became popular topics in the early nineteenth century that saw a surge in publications directed at women's household management. See Lydia Maria Child, *The Frugal Housewife* (New York, 1803), and Child, *The American Frugal Housewife* (1828); Barnard, *Dialogues*; *Experienced American Housekeeper* (Hartford, 1829); Susan Geib discusses changes in work patterns in another Worcester County town for this period in "'Changing Works': Agriculture and Society in Brookfield, Mass., 1785–1820" (Ph.D. diss., Boston Univ., 1981).

45. Robert B. Thomas, *Farmer's Almanac* (Boston: Manning and Loring, 1799).

46. Thomas, *Farmer's Almanac* (Boston: Manning and Loring, 1807).

47. Hitchcock, *Farmer's Friend,* 49.

48. Barnard, *Dialogues,* 13. Mrs. Barnard did not entirely fault the women. She also advocated legislation that would force a husband to hand over his affairs to a conservator before he could impoverish his wife and children.

49. Prude, *Coming of Industrial Order,* especially chap. 2 and pp. 58–63, for the rise in non-textile industries.

50. Figures for 1820 are from the 1820 Federal Decennial Census, which counted persons engaged in various pursuits such as agriculture and manufacturing. Numbers of farmers in 1830 are derived from the 1830 town tax valuations; number engaged in manufacturing is derived from the Secretary of the Treasury's [Louis McLane] *Documents Relative to the Manufactures in the United States,* vol. 1 (Washington: Duff and Green, 1833), doc. no. 308.

51. Peter Whitney, *The History of the County of Worcester* (1793; rpt., Worcester, Mass.: Isaiah Thomas Books and Prints, 1983), 96.

52. Benedict and Tracy, *History of Sutton,* 526–27; Whitney, *History of the County of Worcester,* 96.

53. Conclusions drawn from genealogical and occupational information supplied in Benedict and Tracy on individuals engaged in scythe-making. Benedict and Tracy, *History of Sutton,* 186, 361, 532, 541.

54. Information on Woodbury is as yet incomplete, but this much has been gleaned from Benedict and Tracy, *History of Sutton,* 532, 756; Sutton Valuation and Tax List, 1830; McLane, *Documents,* doc. no. 308.

55. McLane, *Documents,* doc. no. 308.

56. Sutton Valuation and Tax Lists, 1830, 1835.

57. *Centennial History of the Town of Millbury, Massachusetts* (Worcester, Mass.: Davis Press, 1915).

58. Benedict and Tracy, *History of Sutton,* 536.

59. Ibid., 370, 537, 699. Information on Joshua Armsby is also extracted from the Sutton Valuation and Tax Lists, 1830, 1835, 1841, 1845.

60. Benedict and Tracy, *History of Sutton,* 417.

61. Ibid., 391, 399, 404, 531.

62. Maps of Sutton, 1831, 1857. Benedict and Tracy, *History of Sutton,* 531–32.

63. McLane, *Documents,* doc. no. 308.

64. On outwork systems see Thomas Dublin, *Women at Work: The Transformation of Work and Community in Lowell, Massachusetts, 1826–1860* (New York:

Columbia Univ. Press, 1979); Dublin, "Women and Outwork," 51–69; Prude, *Coming of Industrial Order,* chap. 3.

65. Prude, *Coming of Industrial Order,* chap. 2.

66. Ibid.

67. Sutton Valuation and Tax Lists, 1830, 1841. I cannot yet account for the discrepancy in the number of shops reported in the local tax lists, and the numbers reported in the Worcester County Decennial Valuation Record Book. The Decennial Valuation contains much higher shop numbers. All numbers used here were gleaned from the Sutton tax lists.

68. Benedict and Tracy, *History of Sutton,* 265.

69. Nineteen, or 79 percent, of the twenty-four shop-owning farmers owned horses. Eleven, or 45 percent, of the twenty-four also owned chaises. It seems unlikely that anyone who could afford a pleasure horse could not also afford a chaise, and so I am assuming for now that the eight who owned horses without chaises were using those animals for work.

70. All physical description is from fieldwork conducted by the author.

71. Benedict and Tracy, *History of Sutton,* 255.

72. Ibid., 524.

Conclusion

1. Dwight, *Travels,* 1:132, 266; 2:179.

2. *New England Farmer* 8, no. 12 (Oct. 9, 1829): 94.

3. On the separation of home and work and the popularity of the urban ell house, see, for example, Richard Candee, "Landscapes of Expectation: Building, Rebuilding, and Industry in Portsmouth, New Hampshire, 1790–1850," paper presented at Vernacular Architecture Forum Conference, Portsmouth, N.H., 1992; on separation of home and work see Betsy Blackmar, "Rewalking the 'Walking City': Housing and Property Relations in New York City, 1780–1840," ed. Robert Blair St. George, *Material Life in America, 1600–1860* (Boston: Northeastern Univ. Press, 1988), 371–84.

4. *New England Farmer* 1, no. 6 (Sept. 7, 1822): 47.

5. *New England Farmer* 7, no. 25 (Jan. 9, 1829): 195.

6. Henry Ward Beecher, *Norwood; or Village Life in New England* (Charles Scribner, 1868), 215.

7. Charles Dickens, *American Notes, for General Circulation* (London: Chapman and Hall, 1850), 49; Ranlett, *Architect,* 1: 12, 21, 35.

8. See descriptions in Bernard L. Herman, "Architectural and Social Topography of Nineteenth-Century Portsmouth, New Hampshire," in *Gender, Class, and Shelter: Perspectives in Vernacular Architecture* 5, ed. Elizabeth Cromley and Carter Hudgins (Knoxville: Univ. of Tennessee Press, 1995), 225–39; and "'An Old Town By the Sea.'"

Select Bibliography

Primary Sources

Allen, Lewis F. *Rural Architecture.* New York: C. M. Saxton, 1853.

American Husbandry: Containing an Account of the Soil, Climate, Production, and Agriculture of the British Colonies. London: J. Bew, 1775. Rpt., ed. H. J. Carmen and R. G. Tugwell, New York: Columbia Univ. Press, 1939.

Bannister, Rev. James. "On Architecture." Parts 1 and 2. *Massachusetts Magazine* 1 (June/July 1789): 365–66, 401–3.

Barnard, Hannah. *Dialogues on Domestic and Rural Economy.* 1820. Dated pamphlets, American Antiquarian Society, Worcester, Mass.

Beecher, Henry Ward. *Norwood, or, Village Life in New England.* New York: Charles Scribner, 1868.

Benedict, William A., and Hiram A. Tracy, comps. *History of the Town of Sutton, 1704–1876.* Worcester: Sanford, 1878.

Benjamin, Asher. *The American Builder's Companion: or, a System of Architecture: Particularly Adapted to the Present Style of Building.* 6th ed. Boston: R. P. and C. Williams, 1827. Rpt., New York.: Dover Publications, 1969.

Biddle, Owen. *An Improved and Enlarged Edition of Biddle's Carpenter's Assistant,* ed. John Haviland. Philadelphia: M. Polock, 1858.

Bigelow, Lewis. *Address Delivered Before the Worcester Agricultural Society, October 12, 1820.* Worcester, Mass.: Manning and Trumbell, 1821.

Chamberlain, N. H. *A Paper on New England Architecture Read Before the New-England Historic and Genealogical Society, September 4, 1858.* Boston: Crosby, Nichols, 1858.

Chastellux, Marquis de. *Travels in North America, in the years 1780–81–82.* New York, 1828.

Child, Lydia Maria. *The Frugal Housewife dedicated to those who are not ashamed of economy.* 6th ed. Boston: Carter, Hendee and Babcock, 1831.

Cleveland, Henry. "American Architecture." *North American Review* 43 (1836): 356–84.

Coleman, Henry. *An Address before the Hampshire, Franklin, and Hampden Agriculture Society.* Greenfield, Mass.: Phelps and Ingersoll, 1833.

Deane, Samuel. *New England Farmer: or Georgical Dictionary.* 3rd ed. Boston: Wells and Lilly, 1822.

Denny, Samuel. *The Farmer: A Practical Treatise on Agriculture.* Brookfield, Mass.: E. and G. Merriam, 1824.

Dickens, Charles. *American Notes for General Circulation.* 2nd ed. London: Chapman and Hall, 1850.

Downing, Alexander Jackson. *Rural Essays.* Ed. George William Curtis. New York: George P. Putnam, 1853.

Dunlap, William. *History of the Rise and Progress of the Arts of Design in the United States.* 2 vols. New York: George P. Scott, 1834.

Dwight, Timothy. *Travels in New England and New York.* 4 vols. 1822. Rpt., ed. Barbara Miller Solomon, Cambridge: Harvard Univ. Press, Belknap Press, 1969.

Eliot, Jared. *Essays upon Field Husbandry in New England, and Other Papers, 1748–1762.* Ed. Harry J. Carman, Rexford G. Tugwell, and Rodney H. True. New York: Columbia Univ. Press, 1934.

Elsam, Richard. *An Essay on Rural Architecture.* London: St. George's Fields Philanthropic Society, 1803.

————. *Hints for Improving the Condition of the Peasantry in all parts of the United Kingdom, by promoting comfort in their Habitation.* London: R. Ackerman, 1816.

The Experienced American Housekeeper, or Domestic Cookery: formed on Principles of Economy. Hartford: Silas Andrus, 1829.

Fessenden, Thomas. *The Complete Farmer and Rural Economist.* Boston: Lilly, Wait and Co.; George C. Barrett: New England Farmer Office, 1834.

Fiske, Nathan. *The Moral Monitor, or a Collection of Essays on Various Subjects.* 2 vols. Worcester, Mass.: Isaiah Thomas, 1801. Dated books, American Antiquarian Society, Worcester, Mass.

Greenough, Horatio. *The Travels, Observations, and Experiences of a Yankee Stonecutter.* New York, 1852. Excerpted in *America Builds: Source Documents in American Architecture and Planning,* ed. Leland Roth, 78–90. New York: Harper and Row, 1983.

History of Worcester County, Massachusetts. Boston: C. F. Jewett, 1879.

Hitchcock, Enos. *The Farmer's Friend: or the History of Mr. Charles Worthy.* Boston: Isaiah Thomas and E. T. Andrews, 1793.

Humphreys, David. *A Discourse on the Agriculture of the State of Connecticut, and the Means of Making it More Beneficial to the State.* New Haven: T. G. Woodward, 1816.

Johnson, Stephen William. *Rural Economy.* New Brunswick, N.Y.: William Elliot, for I. Riley, 1806.

Lafever, Minard. *The Young Builder's General Instructor.* Newark: W. Tuttle, 1829.

[McLane, Louis.] *Documents Relative to the Manufactures of the United States, by the Secretary of the Treasury.* 2 vols. Washington: Duff Green, 1833.

Morris, Robert. *Select Architecture.* 2nd ed. London: Robert Sayer, 1757. Rpt., New York: DaCapo Press, 1973.

Mott, John, and Frank White. Barns of New England. Unpublished survey, 1976–78. Old Sturbridge Village, Research Department, Sturbridge, Mass.

Quincy, Josiah. "An Address Delivered before the Massachusetts Agricultural Society at the Brighton Cattle Show, October 12, 1819." *Massachusetts Agricultural Repository and Journal* 6 (Jan. 1820): 1–15.

Ranlett, William. *The Architect.* 2 vols. Vol. 1, New York: William H. Graham, 1847; vol. 2, New York: Dewitt and Davenport, 1849.

Thomas, Robert B. *The Farmer's Almanac.* Boston: Manning and Loring, 1793–1831.

Tucker, George. "Thoughts of a Hermit—For the Port Folio: On Architecture." *Port Folio* 4 (1814): 559–69.

Tuthill, Mrs. L. C. *History of Architecture.* Philadelphia: Lindsay and Blakestone, 1848. Rpt., New York: Garland, 1988.

Whitney, Peter. *The History of the County of Worcester.* 1793. Rpt., Worcester, Mass.: Isaiah Thomas, 1983.

Worcester County Decennial Valuations, Worcester County, Mass. Papers, 1665–c. 1954, oversize vol. 2, ms., American Antiquarian Society, Worcester, Mass.

Worlidge, John. *Systema Agriculturae, Being the Mystery of Husbandry Discovered and Layd Open.* 2nd ed. 1675. Facsimile, Los Angeles: Sherwin and Freitel, 1970.

Secondary Sources

Balmori, Diana. "Architecture, Landscape, and the Intermediate Structure: Eighteenth-Century Experiments in Mediation." *Journal of the Society of Architectural Historians* 50 (Mar. 1991): 38–56.

Bermingham, Ann. *Landscape and Ideology: The English Rustic Tradition, 1740–1860.* Berkeley: Univ. of California Press, 1986.

Bloch, Ruth. "The Gendered Meanings of Virtue in Revolutionary America." *Signs* 13, no. 1 (Autumn 1987): 37–58.

Bridenbaugh, Carl. *Peter Harrison: First American Architect.* Chapel Hill: Univ. of North Carolina Press, for the Institute of Early American History and Culture, 1949.

Brooke, John L. *The Heart of the Commonwealth: Society and Political Culture in Worcester County, MA, 1713–1861.* Cambridge: Cambridge Univ. Press, 1989.

Brown, Richard D. "The Emergence of Urban Society in Rural Massachusetts, 1760–1820." *Journal of American History* 61 (June 1974): 29–51.

———. *The Strength of a People: The Idea of an Informed Citizenry in America, 1650–1870.* Chapel Hill: Univ. of North Carolina Press, 1996.

Burns, Sarah. *Pastoral Inventions: Rural Life in Nineteenth Century American Art and Culture.* Philadelphia: Temple Univ. Press, 1989.

Bushman, Richard L. "American High-Style and Vernacular Cultures." In *Colonial British America: Essays in the New History of the Early Modern Era,* ed. Jack P. Greene and J. R. Pole. Baltimore: Johns Hopkins Univ. Press, 1984.

———. "A Poet, a Planter, a Nation of Farmers." *Journal of the Early Republic* 19 (Spring 1999): 1–14.

———. *The Refinement of America: Persons, Houses, Cities.* New York: Vintage Books, 1993.

Campbell, Colin. *The Romantic Ethic and the Spirit of Modern Consumerism.* Oxford: Basil Blackwell, 1987.

Candee, Richard. "'An Old Town By the Sea': Urban Landscapes and Vernacular Building in Portsmouth, New Hampshire, 1660–1990." In Field Guide for the Vernacular Architecture Forum Conference, Portsmouth, N.H., 1992.

Chappell, Edward A. "Housing a Nation: The Transformation of Living Standards in Early America." In *Of Consuming Interests: The Style of Life in the Eighteenth Century,* ed. Cary Carson et al. Charlottesville: Univ. of Virginia Press, for the United States Capitol Historical Society, 1994.

Crook, J. Morduant. *The Dilemma of Style: Architectural Ideas from the Picturesque to the Post-Modern.* Chicago: Univ. of Chicago Press, 1987.

Cummings, Abbott Lowell. *The Framed Houses of Massachusetts Bay, 1625–1725.* Cambridge: Harvard Univ. Press, Belknap Press, 1979.

———. *Massachusetts and Its First Period Houses: A Statistical Survey with Summary Abstracts of Structural History and Transcriptions of Building Documents.*

Rpt. from *Architecture in Colonial Massachusetts*, vol. 51, Publications of the Colonial Society of Massachusetts. Rpt., Boston: Colonial Society of Massachusetts, 1979.

Davidson, Cathy N. *Revolution and the Word: The Rise of the Novel in America.* New York: Oxford Univ. Press, 1986.

Deetz, James. *In Small Things Forgotten: The Archaeology of Early American Life.* New York: Anchor Books, 1977.

Downing, Antoinette F., and Vincent Scully Jr. *The Architectural Heritage of Newport, Rhode Island, 1640–1915.* New York: American Legacy Press, 1967.

Dublin, Thomas. "Women and Outwork in a Nineteenth-Century New England Town: Fitzwilliam, New Hampshire, 1830–1850." In *The Countryside in the Age of Capitalist Transformation: Essays in the Social History of Rural America,* ed. Steven Hahn and Jonathan Prude. Chapel Hill: Univ. of North Carolina Press, 1985.

———. *Women at Work: The Transformation of Work and Community in Lowell, Massachusetts, 1826–1860.* New York: Columbia Univ. Press, 1979.

Eitner, L. E. A., ed. *Neoclassicism and Romanticism, 1750–1850.* 2 vols. Englewood Cliffs, N.J.: Prentice Hall, 1970.

Elkins, Stanley, and Eric McKitrick. *The Age of Federalism: The Early American Republic, 1788–1800.* New York: Oxford Univ. Press, 1993.

Ellis, Joseph. *After the Revolution: Profiles of Early American Culture.* New York: W. W. Norton, 1979

Forbes, Harriet M. "Elias Carter, Architect, of Worcester, Massachusetts." *Old Time New England* 11 (1920): 59–71.

Garrison, J. Ritchie. *Landscape and Material Life in Franklin County, Massachusetts, 1770–1860.* Knoxville: Univ. of Tennessee Press, 1991.

———. "Rebuilding the Barn: Landscape, Barns and Outbuildings in Franklin County, Massachusetts, 1770–1870." Paper presented at Historic Deerfield Colloquium, Deerfield, Mass., Apr. 1991.

Geib, Susan. "'Changing Works': Agriculture and Society in Brookfield, Massachusetts, 1785–1820." Ph.D. diss., Boston Univ., 1981.

Glassie, Henry. "Barns across Southern England: A Note on Transatlantic Comparison and Architectural Meanings." *Pioneer America* 7 (1975): 9–19.

———. "The Variation of Concepts within Tradition: Barn Building in Otsego County, New York." In *Man and Cultural Heritage: Papers in Honor of Fred B. Kniffen,* ed. H. J. Walker and W. G. Haag. Off-set print from *Geoscience and Man* 5 (June 1972): 177–235.

Gross, Robert. "Culture and Cultivation: Agriculture and Society in Thoreau's Concord." *Journal of American History* 69 (June 1982): 42–61.

Hammond, Charles A. "'Where the Arts and Virtues Unite': Country Life Near Boston, 1637–1864." Ph.D. diss., Boston Univ., 1982.

Harris, Neil. "The Making of an American Culture: 1750–1800." In *American Art, 1750–1800: Towards Independence,* ed. Charles Montgomery and Patricia Kane. Boston: New York Graphic Society, 1976.

Herman, Bernard. "The Architectural and Social Topography of Early-Nineteenth-Century Portsmouth, New Hampshire." In *Gender, Class, and Shelter: Perspectives in Vernacular Architecture,* ed. Elizabeth Cromley and Carter L. Hudgins. Vol. 5. Knoxville: Univ. of Tennessee Press, 1995.

———. *Architecture and Rural Life in Central Delaware, 1700–1900.* Knoxville: Univ. of Tennessee Press, 1987.

Honour, Hugh. *Neoclassicism.* New York: Penguin Books, 1977.

Hubka, Thomas. *Big House, Little House, Back House, Barn: The Connected Farm Buildings of New England.* Hanover, N.H.: Univ. of New England Press, 1984.

Jaffee, David. *People of the Wachusett: Greater New England in History and Memory, 1630–1860.* Ithaca: Cornell Univ. Press, 1999.

Johnstone, Paul H. "In Praise of Husbandry." *Agricultural History* 11 (Apr. 1937): 80–95.

———. "Turnips and Romanticism." *Agricultural History* 12 (July 1938): 224–55.

Kelly, J. Frederick. *Early Domestic Architecture of Connecticut.* 1924. Rpt., New York: Dover Publications, 1963.

Kimball, Fiske. *Domestic Architecture of the American Colonies and of the Early Republic.* 1922. Rpt., New York: Dover Publications, 1966.

———. *Mr. Samuel McIntire, Carver, the Architect of Salem.* Portland, Maine: Southworth-Anthoensen Press, 1940.

Kirker, Harold, and James Kirker. *Bulfinch's Boston, 1787–1817.* New York: Oxford Univ. Press, 1964.

Kulik, Gary. "Dams, Fish, and Farmers: Defense of Public Rights in Eighteenth-Century Rhode Island." In *The Countryside in the Age of Capitalist Transformation,* ed. Stephen Hahn and Jonathan Prude. Chapel Hill: Univ. of North Carolina Press, 1985.

Lindgren, James M. *Preserving Historic New England: Preservation, Progressivism, and the Remaking of Memory.* New York: Oxford Univ. Press, 1995.

Low, Anthony. *The Georgic Revolution.* Princeton: Princeton Univ. Press, 1985.

Machin, R. "The Great Rebuilding: A Reassessment." *Past and Present* 77 (Nov. 1977): 33–56.

Marx, Leo. *The Machine in the Garden: Technology and the Pastoral Ideal in America.* New York: Oxford Univ. Press, 1984.

Miller, Marla. "Labor and Liberty in the Age of Refinement: Gender, Class, and the Built Environment." Paper delivered at the Vernacular Architecture Forum Conference, Duluth, Minn., June 2000.

Pocock, J. G. A. "Virtue and Commerce in the Eighteenth Century." *Journal of Interdisciplinary History* 3 (1972): 119–34.

Prown, Jules David. "Style in American Art, 1750–1800." In *American Art, 1750–1800: Towards Independence,* ed. Charles Montgomery and Patricia Kane. Boston: New York Graphic Society, 1976.

Prude, Jonathan. *The Coming of Industrial Order: Town and Factory Life in Rural Massachusetts, 1810–1860.* Cambridge: Cambridge Univ. Press, 1985.

Pruitt, Bettye Hobbs. "Self-Sufficiency and the Agricultural Economy of Eighteenth-Century Massachusetts." *William and Mary Quarterly* 61 (July 1984): 333–64.

Quinan, Jack. "Asher Benjamin and American Architecture." *Journal of the Society of Architectural Historians* 38 (Oct. 1979): 241–61.

Robinson, John Martin. *Georgian Model Farms: A Study of Decorative and Model Farm Buildings in the Age of Improvement, 1700–1846.* Oxford: Clarendon Press, 1983.

Rothenberg, Winifred. *From Market-Places to a Market Economy: The Transformation of Rural Massachusetts, 1750–1850.* Chicago: Univ. of Chicago Press, 1992.

Shipman, William D. "The Federal Style: From About 1790–1825." In *Maine Forms of American Architecture,* ed. Deborah Thompson. Camden, Maine: Downeast Magazine, for the Colby Museum of Art, 1976.

St. George, Robert B. "'Set Thine House in Order': The Domestication of the Yeomanry in Seventeenth-Century New England." In *New England Begins: The Seventeenth Century,* ed. Jonathan Fairbanks and Robert Trent. Vol. 1. Boston: Museum of Fine Arts, 1982.

———. "The Stanley-Lake Barn in Topsfield, Massachusetts: Some Comments on Agricultural Buildings in Early New England." In *Perspectives in Vernacular Architecture,* ed. Camille Wells. Vol. 1. Annapolis, Md.: Vernacular Architecture Forum, 1982.

Steinitz, Michael. "Landmark and Shelter: Domestic Architecture in the Cultural Landscape of the Central Uplands of Massachusetts in the Eighteenth Century." Ph.D. diss., Clark Univ., 1988.

———. "Rethinking Geographical Approaches to the Common House: The Evidence from Eighteenth-Century Massachusetts." In *Perspectives in Vernacular*

Architecture, ed. Thomas Carter and Bernard L. Herman. Vol. 3. Columbia: Univ. of Missouri Press, 1989.

Sweeney, Kevin. "High-Style Vernacular: Lifestyles of the Colonial Elite." In *Of Consuming Interests: The Style of Life in the Eighteenth Century,* ed. Cary Carson et al. Charlottesville: Univ. Press of Virginia, for the United States Capitol Historical Society, 1994.

———. "Mansion People: Kinship, Class, and Architecture in Western Massachusetts in the Mid-Eighteenth Century." *Winterthur Portfolio* 19 (Winter 1984): 231–55.

Swierenga, Robert P. "Theoretical Perspectives on the New Rural History: From Environmentalism to Modernization." *Agricultural History* 56 (1982): 495–502.

Taylor, Alan. *Liberty Men and Great Proprietors: The Revolutionary Settlement on the Maine Frontier, 1760–1820.* Chapel Hill: Univ. of North Carolina Press, for the Institute of Early American History and Culture, 1990.

———. *William Cooper's Town: Power and Persuasion on the Frontier of the Early American Republic.* New York: Vintage Books, 1995.

Thornton, Tamara P. *Cultivating Gentlemen: The Meaning of Country Life among the Boston Elite, 1785–1860.* New Haven: Yale Univ. Press, 1989.

Upton, Dell. "Pattern-Books and Professionalism: Aspects of the Transformation of Domestic Architecture in America, 1800–1860." *Winterthur Portfolio* 19 (Summer/Autumn 1984): 107–50.

———. "Vernacular Domestic Architecture in Eighteenth-Century Virginia." *Winterthur Portfolio* 17 (Summer/Autumn 1982): 95–119.

———. "White and Black Landscapes in Eighteenth-Century Virginia." In *Material Life in America, 1600–1860,* ed. Robert B. St. George. Boston: Northeastern Univ. Press, 1988.

Wenger, Mark. "Architecture and Privacy in Early Virginia." Paper delivered at Vernacular Architecture Forum Conference, Annapolis, Md., May 1998.

Wood, Gordon. *The Radicalism of the American Revolution.* New York: Alfred A. Knopf, 1992.

Wood, Joseph. *The New England Village.* Baltimore: Johns Hopkins Univ. Press, 1997.

Index

Beauty & Convenience was designed and typeset on a Macintosh computer system using QuarkXPress software. The body text is set in 10.5/13.5 Adobe Garamond and display type is set in Americana. This book was designed and typeset by Cheryl Carrington and manufactured by Thomson-Shore, Inc.